MICHELLE GINES

Girl
MAKE-UP YOUR MIND

A BEAUTY INFUSED GUIDE TO PERSONAL GROWTH
7 LESSONS FROM YOUR MAKE-UP BAG

Foreword by Kenyata Gant - CEO, Pink Lipps Cosmetics

Girl, Make Up Your Mind
A Beauty-Infused Guide to Personal Growth
7 Lessons from Your Makeup Bag

Copyright © 2024 by Michelle Gines

Purpose Publishing
13194 US 301 S #417
Riverview, FL 33578

All rights reserved. No part of this publication may be reproduced, distributed, or transmitted in any form or by any means, including photocopying, recording, or other electronic or mechanical methods, without the prior written permission of the publisher, except in the case of brief quotations embodied in critical reviews and certain other noncommercial uses permitted by copyright law.

For permission requests, contact: Purpose Publishing via email at contactus@purposepublishing.com. For speaking engagements, interviews, bulk orders, or promotions contact the author at michelle@michellegines.online.

This book is designed to provide accurate and authoritative information regarding the subject matter covered. It is sold with the understanding that the author or publisher is not engaged in rendering professional services. If professional advice or other expert assistance is required, the services of a competent professional should be sought.

International Standard Book Number 979-8-218-10408-5
Printed in USA
Cover design by Thaddeus Jordan
Interior design by Purpose Publishing

Praises for
Girl, Make Up Your Mind

"Girl, Make Up Your Mind" is a unique and captivating book that beautifully blends the world of makeup with personal development. Michelle Gines offers readers an inspiring journey through the chapters, cleverly structured around makeup bag essentials. While the makeup metaphors grab your attention, the valuable life lessons within will keep you engaged and empowered.

P. Horne, LCSW

In "Cleansing the Beautiful Canvas," Gines invites us to let go of the energy wasted on self-doubt and unmet dreams, setting the stage for a powerful transformation. Each chapter follows, offering insightful guidance on setting boundaries, choosing our mood, and ignoring negativity. Gines empower us to overcome self-sabotage, shed excuses, and set clear intentions for the future.

Shelly Bartolotto, Heart Coach

What makes this book truly special is that it's not just about words on paper. Gines backs up her wisdom with a real-life makeup bag that you can fill with personally curated essentials from the boss herself, Kenyata Gant, of Pink Lipps Cosmetics. These beauty products enhance not only your external appearance but also your internal radiance. It's a delightful and practical addition, a book and beauty brand, two powerful women joining forces. It's fabulous and for real!

Sarah Richard, Scuba Diver

"Girl, Make Up Your Mind" is a refreshing take on personal development, using relatable, everyday items to convey profound insights. If you're looking to boost your confidence, set boundaries, and achieve your goals, this book is your go-to guide. It's an engaging, enlightening read that reminds us that just like makeup, we have the power to enhance our lives and embrace our inner beauty. Don't miss the opportunity to explore these transformative lessons and discover the makeup bag essentials that will help you shine inside and out.

Angelina Crawford, Attorney

"Girl, Make Up Your Mind" by Michelle Gines is an empowering and refreshing take on personal development that cleverly uses makeup bag essentials as metaphors for life improvement. The book offers a unique approach to helping readers rediscover their inner strength, build self-confidence, and achieve their dreams while looking and feeling fabulous.

Donna Joy Richards, Educator

Gines' writing is engaging and relatable, making it easy for readers to connect with the concepts presented in each chapter. The use of makeup terminology not only grabs your attention but also offers insightful lessons on personal growth.

Linda Bryant, Architect

The unique approach of using makeup essentials and relatable metaphors creates an enjoyable and memorable reading experience. Michelle Gines's book offers valuable personal development strategies that are accessible and practical for readers from all social classes. The bonus of a real-life makeup bag and essentials set makes the book even more enticing, as it complements the empowering lessons shared within the chapters.

Nichole Scripps, Cosmetologist

If you are looking to revamp your life and personal growth journey while enjoying a fresh and engaging perspective, "Girl, Make Up Your Mind" is must-read. It's not only filled with wisdom and motivation but also provides tangible products to help you look and feel your best. It's an empowering combination of inner and outer beauty.

Emily Archibold, Dietician

With its empowering content and the allure of the makeup essentials set, "Girl, Make Up Your Mind" is a holistic guide to personal development that will inspire readers to embrace their true potential and look fabulous while doing so.

Domonique Rolfe, Media Professional

"Girl, Make Up Your Mind" is an inspiring and empowering guide that cleverly uses makeup bag essentials as metaphors for personal development. Michelle Gines takes readers on a journey through seven transformative chapters, each linked to a step in a makeup routine. With a perfect blend of practical advice and motivational wisdom, this book will help you not only enhance your outer beauty but also your inner strength and confidence.

Leslie Francis, Life Coach

Michelle Gines' book is not just a source of motivation but also a practical guide for personal growth. The unique makeup bag metaphor adds a fun and relatable aspect to the book, making it enjoyable and insightful. Plus, the bonus makeup kit at the end is the perfect cherry on top, offering a tangible reward for your personal development journey.

Jules D., Talent Acquisition Business Partner

"Girl, Make Up Your Mind" is a must-read for those seeking both inner and outer transformation. It's a reminder that, just like makeup, confidence and self-love can enhance your natural beauty, and you have the power to make it happen.

Jasmine Siska, PA-C

And for those looking to enhance their outer beauty as well, you can grab Michelle Gines' "Girl, Make Up Your Mind Bundle Box" at girlmakeupyourmind.com. This Bundle Box includes a Special Edition Autographed Girl, Make Up Your Mind Book, The Transparent Me (Pink Lipps/ GMUYM) Bag, and get your 20% Off Pink Lipps Cosmetics with your purchase of the bundle and all shipped to you in a Bretty Box. So, grab yours, before they're gone. Limited Edition. While Supplies Last. Grab your ***Girl, Make Up Your Mind Bundle Box*** and get ready to embrace your true beauty, inside and out!

Dedication

To every girl who's ever been told that beauty is in the eye of the beholder. **Behold, you are as beautiful as you believe.** Believe how beautiful you are and help encourage others to do the same. This book is beauty infused through belief, inside and out. The makeup is just for the fun of it, play and enjoy.

Contents

Foreword 13

Introducing Girl, Makeup Your Mind
Beauty is a Belief 23

1. **Cleansing the Beautiful Canvas:**
   Reclaiming Your Energy 35

2. **A Firm Foundation of No:**
   Embracing Boundaries and Empowerment 51

3. **Line Your Eyes, Eyes Don't Lie:**
   Choosing Your Mood 65

4. **Blush Honey Hush:**
   Ignoring Negativity and Embracing Fear 79

5. **Mind Your Mount Mascara:**
   Embracing Fear and Conquering
   Self-Sabotage 93

6. **Lipstick Shift:**
   Bidding Farewell to Reasons and Excuses 109

7. **Mirror a Fresh Face Forward:**
   Setting Clear Intentions for Your Life 123

Let's Zip it Up 141

Foreword

Dear Readers,

I am delighted to introduce you to this transformative guide to personal growth, a journey crafted with expertise and care. As a seasoned makeup artist and proud owner of a thriving cosmetic brand for over 12 years, I am eager to share insights that extend beyond beauty into the profound realm of personal development.

In the following pages, you will embark on a journey tailored for every woman. This self-improvement book is not just a guide; it is a companion for those who cherish the transformative power of makeup and understand the daily struggles that come with being a woman. It is a testament to our strength and an invitation to step into a newfound self, confidently.

This book speaks to women who appreciate the artistry of makeup and face the multifaceted challenges of daily life. It is a guide for those seeking not only beauty in the mirror but also beauty in their strength, resilience, and personal growth. Through my years of experience, I have come to realize that true beauty radiates from within, and this guide is designed to illuminate that inner light.

May you find inspiration, encouragement, and practical wisdom as you navigate the pages ahead. Here's to embracing your unique journey, standing tall in your authenticity, and walking confidently in your newness. Let this be the beginning of a transformative adventure where makeup is not just a tool for enhancement but a catalyst for self-discovery and empowerment.

As a makeup artist, I have witnessed the incredible impact that makeup can have on confidence and self-perception. The artistry of makeup extends beyond the surface, delving into the very essence of who we are and who we aspire to be. It is this understanding that forms the foundation of the wisdom shared within these pages.

Reflecting on my journey as a makeup artist and entrepreneur, I am reminded of the countless faces I've had the privilege of working on, each telling a unique story of beauty and resilience. It is this mosaic of experiences that has fuelled my passion for the art of makeup and the empowerment of women.

In the world of cosmetics, I have witnessed not only the physical transformations that makeup can bring but also its profound impact on self-esteem. Makeup is about revealing the inner confidence that may be hidden beneath the surface. This book seeks to bridge the gap between the external and internal, acknowledging that true beauty is a harmonious blend of both.

This guide sets itself apart with a tailored approach to women addressing the unique beauty and challenges they face. As you dive into the chapters ahead, you will encounter practical tips, personal anecdotes, and thought-provoking reflections aimed at nurturing your personal growth journey.

In the tapestry of "Girl; Make Up Your Mind (Beauty is a Belief)," these seven chapters weave together to form a transformative narrative—a journey of self-discovery and empowerment. Each step, a brushstroke on the canvas of your existence, paints a portrait of resilience, authenticity, and intentional living.

As you navigate the 7 incredible mind-shifts and 7 life-altering moves crafted by "Michelly", envision yourself stepping into a realm where true beauty is not merely a reflection in the mirror but a radiant glow illuminating from within. From reclaiming your emotional energy to bidding farewell to excuses, each step is a dance with self-empowerment, a symphony of transformation.

At the end, you stand at the crossroads of self-discovery, armed with the wisdom to choose your mood, embrace opportunities, overcome self-sabotage, and set clear intentions for a purposeful future. These are not mere chapters; they are gateways to a life filled with the beautiful and intentional living.

As you reflect on these transformative moments, anticipate a symphony of transformation. Within these words lies the power to illuminate your world and redefine your understanding of beauty. These are the keys to unlocking the door to your authentic self—a self-adorned with the timeless beauty of self-love and purpose. Embrace these mind-shifts, dance through these life-altering moves, and witness the renaissance of your truest, most beautiful self.

In essence, this book is an ode to the beauty that exists in every woman, transcending the superficial and embracing the strength, resilience, and uniqueness within. May this guide be a compass, guiding you towards a more empowered, confident, and authentic version of yourself.

Warm regards,

Kenyata Gant
Makeup Artist and Founder/CEO of
Pink Lipps Cosmetics

Dear Readers,

Welcome to "Girl; Make Up Your Mind (A Beauty Infused Guide to Personal Growth, 7 Lessons from Your Makeup Bag)," is a transformative guide to personal growth, crafted with expertise and care. As a seasoned makeup artist and proud owner of a thriving cosmetic brand for over 12 years, I am eager to share insights beyond beauty into the profound realm of personal development.

As a makeup artist, I've witnessed the incredible impact that makeup can have on confidence and self-perception. The artistry of makeup delves into the essence of who we are and who we aspire to be, forming the foundation of the wisdom shared within these pages.

Reflecting on my journey as a makeup artist and entrepreneur, I am reminded of the countless faces I've had the privilege of working on, each telling a unique story of beauty and resilience. It is this mosaic of experiences that has fueled my passion for the art of makeup and the empowerment of women.

In the world of cosmetics, I have witnessed not only the physical transformations that makeup can bring but also its profound impact on self-esteem.

Makeup is about revealing the inner confidence that may be hidden beneath the surface. This book seeks to bridge the gap between the external and internal, acknowledging that true beauty is a harmonious blend of both.

In this book, Michelle Gines, speaks to women who appreciate the artistry of makeup and face the multifaceted challenges of daily life. It is a guide for those seeking not only beauty in the mirror but also beauty in their strength, resilience, and personal growth. Through my years of experience, I've come to realize that true beauty radiates from within, and this guide is designed to illuminate that inner light.

May you find inspiration, encouragement, and practical wisdom as you navigate the pages ahead. Here's to embracing your unique journey, standing tall in your authenticity, and walking confidently in your newness. Let this be the beginning of a transformative adventure where makeup is not just a tool for enhancement but a catalyst for self-discovery and empowerment.

In the following pages, embark on a journey tailored for every woman. This self-improvement book is not just a guide; it's a companion for those who cherish the transformative power of makeup and understand the daily struggles that come with being a woman. It's a testament to our strength and an invitation to step into newfound self-confidence.

This guide sets itself apart with a tailored approach to women addressing the unique beauty and challenges they face. As you dive into the chapters ahead, you will encounter practical tips, personal anecdotes, and thought-provoking reflections aimed at nurturing your personal growth journey.

In the tapestry of "Girl; Make Up Your Mind (Beauty is a Belief)," these seven chapters weave together to form a transformative narrative—a journey of self-discovery and empowerment. Each step, a brushstroke on the canvas of your existence, paints a portrait of resilience, authenticity, and intentional living.

As you navigate the 7 incredible mind-shifts and 7 life-altering moves crafted by the persona, "Michelly," envision yourself stepping into a realm where true beauty is not merely a reflection in the mirror but a radiant glow illuminating from within. From reclaiming your emotional energy to bidding farewell to excuses, each step is a dance with self-empowerment, a symphony of transformation.

At the end, you stand at the crossroads of self-discovery, armed with the wisdom to choose your mood, embrace opportunities, overcome self-sabotage, and set clear intentions for a purposeful future. These are not mere chapters; they are gateways to a life filled with beautiful and intentional living.

As you reflect on these transformative moments, anticipate a symphony of transformation. Within these words lies the power to illuminate your world and redefine your understanding of beauty. These are the keys to unlocking the door to your authentic self—a self-adorned with the timeless beauty of self-love and purpose. Embrace these mind-shifts, dance through these life-altering moves, and witness the renaissance of your truest, most beautiful self.

In essence, this book is an ode to the beauty that exists in every woman, transcending the superficial and embracing the strength, resilience, and uniqueness within. May this guide be a compass, guiding you towards a more empowered, confident, and authentic version of yourself.

Warm regards,

Kenyata Gant
Makeup Artist and Founder/CEO of
Pink Lipps Cosmetics

Introducing *Girl*, Makeup Your Mind
Beauty is a Belief

Let me start by introducing you to Girl, Make Up Your Mind. The book, the makeup bag, but more importantly the message. Beauty is a belief, and that belief is in yourself. So, get ready to embark on a whirlwind journey across the globe with me, as I share a message that's tailor-made for women just like you! In this modern age, even I find myself immersed in the world of Zoom meetings, but that's just the tip of the iceberg. Over the past two years, I've authored not one, not two, but six incredible books, including the very one you're holding, which happens to be my very first National Bestseller! Among my clients, I'm renowned for my knack for simplifying complex issues and solving problems.

But here's the real kicker – creating lasting change in your life isn't as tough as it may seem, even if life has tossed you around like a hot potato. I promise you this book is your new, secret weapon.

As you delve into the upcoming chapters, I'm going to shower you with some of my best-kept secrets and reimagined shortcuts for achieving mindset shifts that are not only transformative but downright delectable. It's like savoring your favorite dessert without a hint of guilt – they're zero calories, but they bring heaps of character-boosting change to your life. It's all about living your best life, here and now, with grace and ease.

Hold on, though, I didn't say it would be a walk in the park; shifting your mindset isn't always a cakewalk when you've been dwelling in your head for quite some time. But fret not, because what I'm about to share isn't complicated. The rewards are so game-changing and liberating that you'll be willing to put in the effort.

This journey we're about to embark upon might have its fair share of bumps and stretches, making you feel slightly uncomfortable. It could encourage you to step outside your comfort zone, but I urge you not to close this book. Instead, embrace these feelings and see what invaluable lessons they have to offer.

And yes, there might be some unlearning, unholding, and unhugging to be done along the way. Letting go of things you've outgrown is part of the transformation. Stick around; we'll explore these concepts in more detail.

In the meantime, I encourage you to embrace discomfort because, let's be honest, living an ordinary life is way too easy. Most people are content with "fine" or "okay," but if you want to revel in an abundant, blessed, and fulfilling life. You need to start by being okay with not being just okay.

You've already made a commitment by picking up this book, and it's my commitment to help you achieve your best and most brilliant life.

Throughout this adventure, we'll acknowledge the truth, whether it's good or bad, and we'll embrace it. It's all about turning the tables in your favor. It's time to bring your authentic self to the forefront because that's where the shift begins – how you see yourself and how the world sees you. Get ready for an exhilarating ride!

So, get ready for 7 incredible mindset shifts and 7 life-altering moves. By the end of this journey, ordinary will be a thing of the past. Welcome to "Girl, Make Up Your Mind," a beauty-infused guide to personal growth. Inspired by that magical place where girls often turn to – their makeup bags. This is where we find tools to empower, boast, and gain confidence, but it's also where we camouflage, hide, and sometimes shrink. There's a method to my madness though. In the book you've got

- A Topic/Tool (metaphorical) makeup bag reference.
- The Brain's makeup of how/why it challenges us.
- Practical Self-Coaching Tips to help you overcome it.
- and Michelly's story to impart, inspire, and ignite you.

Meet my friend, Michelly, who's opening her makeup bag and sharing her story at the end of each chapter.

It's the combination of the beauty infusion, common challenges and the love of a good story that's layered in that make it heartwarming. But the authenticity of what really happens in our heads and hearts is what makes this book a game changer to me. And what I believe will be for many others as well. But you be the judge and tell me what you think once you get through it. I think you'll like Michelly and the items in her bag. It's my prayer that like hers, you'll turn your bag into an amazing source of strength for you too.Top of Form

I am using my own creativity and engaging way to structure my book chapters using the handy dandy, makeup bag. It's our essentials and it's just as personal as it is pertinent to our personal development. So, here's the metaphors I have in store for you:

1. **Cleansing Your Beautiful Canvas**: In this chapter, we will dive deep into the concept of letting go of past fantasies, regrets and self-criticism. We will explore how to clean your "canvas" by releasing the energy wasted on unfulfilled dreams and self-doubt. There's a real joy in getting over past regrets and self-criticism. I share

practical exercises and techniques for mental and emotional cleansing.
2. **A Firm Foundation of No**: I'm delving into the power of setting boundaries and learning to say "no" without guilt. We will discuss the importance of a strong foundation for your personal growth journey and how it enables you to build a resilient mindset. Includes strategies for setting healthy boundaries in various aspects of life.
3. **Line Your Eyes, Eyes Don't Lie**: Offer insights into mastering your mood and choosing positivity every day. Explore how our mindset can influence our daily experiences. Readers leave with tools to "line their eyes" with optimism and resilience, regardless of external circumstances. You must see it, so you can be it.
4. **Blush Honey Hush**: Unpack the notion of ignoring negativity and focusing on self-worth. Learn how to overcome fear, self-doubt, and external criticism. Learn how to confront the inner and outer critics head-on, fostering self-confidence and personal growth.

5. **Mind Your Mount Mascara**: Explore how we often self-sabotage our own success and happiness. Includes practical strategies to overcome self-sabotage and clear the path to personal fulfillment. Stop getting in your own way and start pursuing your goals.
6. **Lipstick Shift**: Discuss the significance of eliminating excuses and reasons that hold us back. Includes guidance on how to replace negative self-talk with empowering and action-oriented language. Plus, exercises that embrace a "lipstick shift" in your mindset and with your mouth; words matter.
7. **Mirror a Fresh Face Forward**: Dive into the power of setting clear intentions and goals. Gain guidance on how to shift your focus from what you don't want to what you truly desire. Encourages the development of a vision for the future and guides you in aligning your actions with your aspirations.

Throughout the book, I interweave practical exercises, real-life examples, and personal anecdotes to make the content relatable and actionable. The metaphor of makeup essentials adds a unique and memorable touch to your personal development journey. It's the stuff you use every day or even if not every day, from time to time. You know what they are and why women use them. Whether to touch up or cover up, it's all good.

And, of course, there's a real-life makeup bag with essential products as a fantastic way to engage you as not only a reader, but an action taker. The bag and contents provide you with glamorous, practical tools to enhance your look and your life. Good luck as you dive into the book, and I hope it inspires and empowers many women on their personal growth journeys! Share it with a friend. Give it as a gift. I want you to make sure you go online and tag me at #reImagineYOUniversity as you go along. Join me in the community on Facebook and get your workbook download to accompany the book at michellegines.online.

As you journey through these pages, get ready for a treasure trove of tips, strategies, shortcuts, and real-life stories that will kickstart your transformation. Remember, change isn't about grandiose, one-time acts but a series of small, joyful, and effective shifts you eagerly repeat.

Each chapter will whisk you into a special coaching session featuring individuals who've taken these very steps to revamp their mindset. Their insights and experiences will illuminate the path you're about to embark on. No need for a notebook and pen while reading; I've got you covered with a free, downloadable workbook at www.michellegines.online. It's loaded with key takeaways, exercises, and journal prompts.

And guess what? Your journey doesn't have to be a solitary one. Share your "Aha!" moments, your journey, or even a selfie of your reading spot on Instagram or Facebook, tagging @Re-ImagineYOUniversity and using #MGMentorMe. I can't wait to connect and celebrate your progress with you!

Now, before we dive headfirst into the seven transformative steps, let's revisit a fundamental principle. You see, the key to igniting change lies in cultivating the right mindset before taking action. Here's the simple reason behind it: Your thoughts shape your feelings, which in turn dictate your actions. I call this the "architecture of change," and it forms the bedrock of "Girl, Make Up Your Mind."

While most people initially focus on action, it's merely the final step in a three-part process for sustainable change. Just as an architect considers a building's foundation, walls, and roof as an integrated whole, you need to harmonize your headspace, heart space, and high place. To make lasting change a breeze, these three realms must be considered in unison. As I shared in the beginning, beauty is a belief. You have a beautiful life in front of you and you are the beautiful life within you. Between the two, there is a brain that must be reminded and I'm sharing just a snip right here.

Let's break down these three spaces further:

1. **Headspace: Change Your Thoughts**
   Here's where it all begins—in your mind. Mastering your headspace empowers you to think like a winner, making life's challenges significantly more manageable. Your thoughts wield control over your feelings, and by mastering this domain, you'll spot and banish any self-imposed limits,

blocks, fears, or obstacles long before they obstruct your path. Take command of your thoughts about your goals, dreams, and aspirations, and watch as they seamlessly become reality.

2. **Heart Space: Change Your Feelings**
Your feelings are the puppeteer of your actions. When you gain mastery over your heart space, inspiration and motivation become your natural states of being. Feelings aren't good or bad; what matters is the power you grant them. Instead of expecting constant happiness, you'll learn to embrace a wide range of emotions without letting them steer your life. You'll even harness the ability to conjure new feelings when you need their support.

3. **High Place: Change Your Actions**
Actions are the brick and mortar of change. Mastering your high place makes it a breeze to take the necessary steps toward the change you crave and the results you desire. It's not just about visible actions; it's the invisible decisions and choices that you'll make, transforming the seen into the effortless. With your high place in order,

even the most challenging actions will feel like second nature.

And with that, the adventure begins. Gear up for an exhilarating journey through the seven steps, where ordinary will be a thing of the past, and the extraordinary will become your new normal. Get ready to make over your mindset and emerge as the empowered, confident, and resilient individual you were always meant to be. Starting now.

"Cleansing the canvas of unfulfilled dreams allows you to reclaim your energy and paint the masterpiece of the true you." *MG*

Cleansing the Beautiful Canvas:
Reclaiming Your Energy

Welcome to the first step of your transformation journey: **Cleanse Your Beautiful Canvas**. We're diving headfirst into the territory of your mindset—your "headspace." Buckle up because we're about to unlock the secrets to paving the way for genuine and lasting change.

Remember those days when you were asked, "What do you want to be when you grow up?" It's a fun question with answers ranging from the amusing to the profoundly enlightening. As kids, we don't hold back on our dreams, letting our imagination run wild. But here's the kicker: as teenagers and adults, we often end up just as unrealistic in our aspirations.

Personally, I had two extremes I like to live under one was a teacher and the other was Wonder Woman. I'd spend hours daydreaming, crafting my bulletproof bracelets out of tin foil, ready to vanquish villains with my Lasso of Truth (also fashioned from tin foil). I clung to this dream longer than any reasonable adult should. Even when I realized Wonder Woman was a character portrayed by the fantastic Linda Carter, I didn't fully let go. I merely shifted my focus to becoming a movie star, aspiring to fulfill my dreams on the screen. But the truth is, it was never a dream—it was a fantasy. So, let's deal with fantasy first.

The first step in detoxifying your dreams is to differentiate between dreams and fantasies. I mean, neither of us genuinely believes I could become Diana, Princess of Themyscira. No amount of wishing, hoping, or daydreaming could change that because it was pure fantasy. It's okay to have fantasies in life, if you don't mistake them for dreams.

Fantasies are enjoyable to think about, while dreams are worth chasing.

Now, you might be thinking, "Wait a minute, Michelle, aren't you a Re-Imagine Strategist/Coach? Shouldn't you tell me I can be anything I want, that I have unlimited potential, and that I can achieve anything I believe in?" You're absolutely right—I firmly believe in your boundless potential. But here's the catch: you must be willing to work for it. This may entail hard work, sacrifices, and facing daunting challenges. Sometimes, it means gaining clarity about your goals, understanding whether it's the destination or the journey that truly matters, and whether the prize is worth the effort.

Fantasies are where ideas stagnate, remaining mere thoughts you cherish without acting upon. That's perfectly okay. However, it's important not to confuse fantasies with real dreams, and to avoid beating yourself up for not achieving the unattainable.

Now that we've released our fantasies, let's deal with dreams that never truly belonged to us—the "Coulda, Woulda, Shoulda" dreams. These are the goals we feel expected to achieve but don't necessarily lead to a happy, fulfilling life. When you catch yourself saying, "I could do this," or "I should do that," it's a clear sign you're not pursuing what you genuinely want. These are often the regrets in our lives. Those things we wish we had acted on, but for whatever reason we didn't and now we live with the unrealized unknowns of what could have, should have or would have been. There is a harsh reality to this that you must wake up to and realize and so I'm going to just rip the band aid off now. Move on! There was a window of opportunity at a point in time that you chose not to pursue. Now, if that window were to open again – you can make a different decision. But for the decision that has already been made, it's done. We can't change it now, but you can make peace with the fact that a choice made is a choice made.

The next step is to let go of expectations. Society, our community, family, and friends can heavily influence our lives. Sometimes these expectations are obvious, while others are hidden within. You might have been influenced by family traditions, gender roles, or societal norms that dictated what you should be doing. You might have set goals to impress others, believing it's what's expected of you. Here's where you need to liberate yourself from those expectations, whether they come from you or the world.

Another crucial step is letting go of any pressure resulting from your awareness of your potential. Just because you can achieve something doesn't mean you have to. You may possess the potential to excel in various fields, but that doesn't mean those paths are right for you. Understanding the difference between potential and passion is key. Pursuing something solely because you can doesn't guarantee happiness.

As you cleanse your canvas, you must also ensure that your dreams align with your values. Your values are the principles and priorities that define your life. Sometimes, a dream may not truly align with you but is pursued to please others. When your dreams clash with your values, progress feels like pushing a boulder uphill.

Lastly, be ready to let go of dreams whose time has passed. Just like the food you find lurking at the back of your fridge; some dreams have expiration dates. As life moves on, dreams and values evolve. You need to let go of past ideas to make room for the future.

Don't fall into the trap of clinging to dreams you had when you were younger and assume you will still be chasing them years later. Growing up, our aspirations shift, and what felt right at 18 may not resonate at 25, 45, or 65. It's not about giving up on your dreams; it's about allowing them to evolve naturally.

When you decide to release a dream, don't mistake it for giving up. Instead, think of it as setting yourself free. Just because you once wanted something doesn't mean you're forever bound to it. Your dreams belong to you, and you have the power to release them when they no longer serve your growth.

Finally, redirect your focus away from achieving every single goal and toward living a blessed and fulfilling life. A good life doesn't require every goal to be met or every dream to come true. In fact, it's unrealistic to expect perfection. At the end of your life, what truly matters is whether you've lived in a way that makes you happy and fulfilled. Happiness isn't about achieving every goal; it's about doing what's important to you.

Remember, it's entirely acceptable to let go of a dream that no longer fits your life. No apologies are needed. Life changes, values change, and dreams are allowed to change too. In the end, living a blessed life is different from living a perfect one, and it's a goal within everyone's grasp.

As we conclude our first step, "Cleanse the Canvas," let's reflect on the invaluable lessons we've uncovered in this chapter. I'd also like to share Lakeya's inspirational journey through these lessons.

Lesson 1: Separate Your Dreams from Your Fantasies. Remember, a fantasy is something you enjoy thinking about, while a dream is something you're willing to work towards. This distinction is essential to begin your transformation journey.

Lesson 2: Release Yourself from Expectations. Be it your own or those imposed upon you, it's crucial to free yourself from the weight of expectations, no matter how well-intentioned. Your life's path is uniquely yours.

Lesson 3: Embrace Your Potential but Don't Feel Obligated to Pursue It. Just because you can achieve something doesn't mean you have to. Success is not about conforming to others' expectations but following your own desires.

Lesson 4: Align Dreams with Your Values. To achieve genuine happiness, ensure your dreams support the values that matter most to you. Pursue goals that bring you closer to what truly matters in life.

Lesson 5: Discard Expired Dreams. Just as that forgotten item at the back of the fridge is tossed out, let go of dreams that no longer fit your life. Change is natural, and your dreams can evolve with you.

Lesson 6: Accept That Dreams Can Change. Life changes, values change, and so can your dreams. It's not a reflection of failure but a part of growth and evolution.

Lesson 7: Prioritize a Blessed and Fulfilling Life. At the heart of it all, remember that the number of goals achieved doesn't define your happiness. What truly matters is living a life that feels blessed and fulfilling to you.

Lakeya's journey beautifully encapsulates these lessons. For years, she felt pressured to obtain multiple degrees to prove her worth. Her unfinished MBA began to loom over her, even as she transitioned through various life stages. She realized that it was time to let go of this outdated dream. Her newfound understanding allowed her to embrace her worth, talents, and competence. She valued herself more than any piece of paper.

And there you have it—our first step in the transformation journey. Let Lakeya's experience serve as inspiration as we move forward.

Don't forget to download the accompanying workbook from michellegines.online. In the next chapter, we'll explore "A Firm Foundation" and show you how to discover your "NO." You'll learn to create a new mindset that supports your boundaries, making it easier to say no when needed, and freeing you from guilt and recriminations that often accompany it. Stay tuned for the next exciting installment of your journey to transformation.

Make Up of the Brain – Cleansing the Canvas

Focusing on regrets and self-criticism cannot help you because it keeps you stuck in the past, preventing personal growth and happiness. When you dwell on mistakes and constantly criticize yourself, it creates a negative mindset that can lead to anxiety and low self-esteem, making it harder to move forward and achieve your goals. It's like carrying a heavy burden that weighs you down and prevents you from enjoying the present and building a better future.

There are brain mechanisms and psychological factors that can contribute to a tendency to focus on regret and self-criticism. Some of these include:

1. **Rumination:** The brain tends to replay past events and mistakes, often dwelling on negative experiences. This is known as rumination, and it can reinforce self-criticism and regret.
2. **Negative Bias:** The brain is wired to give more attention to negative information as a survival mechanism. This can lead people to magnify their mistakes and dwell on regrets.
3. **Amygdala Activation:** The amygdala, a region in the brain associated with processing emotions, can become overac-

tive in response to negative self-evaluation, amplifying feelings of regret and self-criticism.
4. **Social Comparison:** People tend to compare themselves to others, which can lead to feelings of inadequacy and self-criticism if they perceive themselves as falling short in comparison.
5. **Memory Consolidation:** The brain tends to store emotionally charged memories more effectively. If you have strong negative emotions associated with past regrets, they may be more accessible in your memory.

It's important to be aware of these factors and practice techniques like mindfulness, self-compassion, and cognitive reframing to counteract the brain's natural inclination to focus on regret and self-criticism.

3 Practical Exercises – Cleansing the Canvas

Overcome past regrets, detoxify dreams and self-criticism

1. **Gratitude Journaling:**
   - Keep a gratitude journal. Each day, encourage them to write down three things you are grateful for.
   - Reflect on both small and significant positive experiences from their day.
   - Over time, this exercise can shift your focus from regrets and self-criticism to positive aspects of your life, promoting a more optimistic outlook.

2. **Positive Affirmations:**
   - Use positive affirmations. Identify your most common self-critical thoughts and replace them with positive, affirming statements.
   - Encourage yourself by repeating these affirmations regularly, especially when self-criticism or regretful thoughts arise.

- This practice helps rewire your thought patterns towards self-compassion and self-acceptance.

3. **Constructive Self-Reflection:**
    - Practice constructive self-reflection by setting aside a specific time each week to review your past actions and decisions.

"The Unveiling Wipe"

Michelly had always been the kind of person who harbored countless unfulfilled dreams and was plagued by self-doubt. She had a makeup bag filled with various items, each serving as a reminder of her aspirations. But there was one item in her bag that held a special power, a cleansing wipe that she had received as a free sample from a cosmetics store.

One evening, after a particularly disheartening day at work, Michelly decided to do a bit of self-care. She rummaged through her makeup bag, searching for her favorite lipstick, but her hand landed on the cleansing wipe instead. Curiosity got the better of her, and she decided to use it. She wiped away the layers of makeup, revealing her bare face.

As she wiped away the last traces of mascara and foundation, something extraordinary happened. The cleansing wipe seemed to exude a soft, ethereal glow, and Michelly's reflection in the mirror began to change. She saw a younger version of herself, full of hopes and dreams, staring back at her. It was as if the wipe was not just removing makeup but also the layers of self-doubt and unfulfilled aspirations that had accumulated over the years.

In this magical moment, Michelly was transported back in time to pivotal moments in her life. She watched as her younger self pursued her passions, daring to dream and strive for greatness. She saw the precise moments when self-doubt had crept in, holding her back from achieving her goals. The cleansing wipe allowed her to witness her journey and the energy she had wasted on self-doubt and unfulfilled dreams.

As she moved through these memories, Michelly felt a surge of emotions. She confronted her past regrets and the opportunities she had let slip through her fingers. Her younger self turned to her, as if seeking guidance. With a newfound sense of determination, Michelly whispered words of encouragement to herself, urging her younger self to believe in her abilities and to pursue her dreams with unwavering confidence.

As the memories played out, the cleansing wipe absorbed the energy of Michelly's past self-doubt and regrets. When the journey through time was complete, Michelly returned to her reflection in the mirror. This time, she looked at herself with a sense of understanding and self-assurance. The makeup bag item had served as a vessel to release the energy she had wasted on unfulfilled dreams and self-doubt.

With a heart full of renewed purpose, Michelly put the cleansing wipe back in her makeup bag, no longer just an item but a powerful reminder of her inner strength. She knew that her journey was far from over, but she was ready to face it with the confidence she had found within herself. The cleansing wipe had not only revealed her true self but had also given her the courage to pursue her dreams once more.

"Setting boundaries is a way of caring for myself. It doesn't make me mean, selfish, or uncaring, because I don't do it to other people. I do it to take care of me." - Unknown

A Firm Foundation of No:
Embracing Boundaries and Empowerment

Are you constantly racing to meet everyone else's needs, leaving no time or energy for yourself? It's time for you to discover the magic of "No." Not now, not ever, and definitely not at the cost of your own happiness. By the end of this chapter, you'll be equipped with the knowledge to set and maintain clear boundaries while saying "No" without the weight of guilt or regret. So, let's dive right in!

Think back to your toddler days when "no" was one of your first words, and you wielded it with unwavering authority. But as you grew into adulthood, that power diminished. You found yourself saying "yes" more than you should have, often to your detriment. Picture this: you're running in a thousand different directions, catering to everyone's needs, but there's nothing left for you. You're left feeling drained, resentful, and frustrated. Sound familiar?

The good news is learning how to establish and uphold your boundaries can transform your perspective. This chapter will equip you to shift your mindset and reclaim your right to say "no" when necessary, without the baggage of guilt or judgment.

Mindset Shift 1: Prioritize Self-Interest Over Selfishness. It's not selfish to put your needs first; it's an act of self-interest. Being selfish is when you disregard others for your gain, but putting your needs in their rightful place isn't selfish—it's self-care. Recognize that your needs deserve recognition, consideration, and accommodation.

Mindset Shift 2: Press Pause on Your Response. Don't let the pressure of immediate responses force you into unwanted commitments. Take time to reflect. If someone demands an answer right away, train yourself to pause, whether it's for minutes, hours, or even days. This simple act grants you space to consider your true feelings and make an informed decision.

Mindset Shift 3: Don't Always Jump When Asked. Just because someone makes a request doesn't mean you must drop everything and comply immediately. Learn from an unexpected source, like my local dry cleaner, who gracefully navigated customer expectations. Align your assistance with your schedule and resources, not just theirs.

Mindset Shift 4: Embrace "I Don't Want To" as a Valid Reason. You don't need an elaborate justification for saying "no." If you don't want to do something, that's reason enough to decline. No explanations or apologies are necessary. Not every request aligns with your desires, and that's perfectly okay.

Mindset Shift 5: Others' Reactions Aren't Your Responsibility. When you say "no," anticipate that not everyone will be pleased with your decision. It's normal for people to feel disappointed or dissatisfied when their requests are declined. However, these reactions belong to them, not you. Stick to your firm stance while respecting their feelings.

Mindset Shift 6: Avoid Letting Feelings Rule Your Decisions. Many feel compelled to say "yes" due to guilt, expectation, or the fear of judgment. When you're tempted to answer affirmatively out of these emotions, ask yourself why you feel this way. Analyze whether the obligation stems from a genuine necessity or societal expectations.

Redefine your expectations and transform the way you live your life. Setting clear boundaries and confidently saying "no" will liberate you. No more feeling overwhelmed and trapped by others' demands. Claim your right to prioritize your own needs and remember that you are responsible for your well-being and happiness.

Stay tuned for the accompanying workbook at Michellegines.online, where you can explore practical tips for implementing these mindset shifts in your daily life. You're on your way to mastering the art of "No" and living a life that's truly yours.

Imagine living a life where your decisions are aligned with your values, and your inner needs are as important as anyone else's. This chapter delves into the transformational power of saying "No" and provides you with valuable insights to empower your personal and professional life.

During our coaching session, I had the pleasure of speaking with Alanna, a 37-year-old beauty consultant who unveiled her lightbulb moment while navigating the art of discovering her "No." Alanna, like many, had the habit of saying "yes" when she should have been saying "no." She was known for accommodating others, avoiding drama or friction, even at the expense of her own well-being. Whether it was taking on more clients than she could handle, juggling numerous social commitments, or adjusting her work hours to accommodate clients worldwide in different time zones, she was caught in the "disease to please."

Alanna shared her realization that she didn't have to prioritize everyone else's needs over her own. She recognized the importance of setting boundaries and valuing her time and well-being. For work-related meetings scheduled at inconvenient hours, she learned to negotiate and find mutually agreeable times. The same principles applied to her social life; she decided not to silently rearrange her schedule to accommodate friends. Alanna's newfound understanding was liberating. She began making herself a priority by scheduling time each day for self-care activities.

To conclude this chapter and recap its most important takeaways:

1. **Prioritize Self-Interest Over Selfishness:** Saying "no" doesn't make you selfish; it signifies that your needs matter too.
2. **Press Pause on Your Response:** Give yourself time to consider whether your answer should be "yes" or "no." Don't feel pressured to decide immediately.
3. **Don't Always Jump When Asked:** Don't be at everyone's beck and call. If you decide to accommodate someone's request, do it on your terms.

4. **Define Your Boundaries:** People will only take advantage of you if you allow them. Set clear boundaries for your time and energy.
5. **"I Don't Want To" is a Valid Reason:** You don't need an elaborate justification. If you don't want to do something, that's reason enough.
6. **Others' Reactions Aren't Your Responsibility:** Disappointment is a natural reaction when you say "no." However, their feelings are theirs to manage, not yours.
7. **Don't Let Feelings Rule Your Decisions:** Recognize that many obligations are driven by societal expectations. Reevaluate these and prioritize your own needs and values.

With these insights, you're well on your way to mastering the art of "No" and liberating yourself from the shackles of overcommitment and people-pleasing.

In our next chapter, "Step Three: Line the Eyes that Don't Lie," we'll dive into the process of creating each day as a good day, regardless of external circumstances. You have the power to choose your mood and how you experience each day. Decide that today will be a good day and take the steps to make it your reality.

Make Up of the Brain – A Firm Foundation of No

Feeling guilty for setting boundaries can hurt you because it can lead to self-neglect and stress. When you feel guilty, you may avoid taking care of your own needs and end up overextending yourself to please others. This can cause burnout, resentment, and a decline in your overall well-being, as you prioritize others' needs over your own. Setting boundaries is essential for maintaining a healthy balance in relationships and self-care, and guilt can hinder this important self-preservation

There are psychological and neurological factors that can contribute to feelings of guilt when setting boundaries or saying no. Some of these include:

1. **Social Conditioning:** From an early age, people are often conditioned to be polite, helpful, and considerate of others' needs. Saying no or setting boundaries may feel

like violating these social norms, triggering feelings of guilt.
2. **Empathy:** Many people are naturally empathetic, which means they are attuned to the emotions and needs of others. This can lead to a fear of hurting or disappointing others when setting boundaries, causing guilt.
3. **Neurological Response:** When you anticipate conflict or disapproval from others, the brain's stress response may be activated. This can include the release of stress hormones, which can intensify feelings of guilt.
4. **Self-Worth:** People often tie their self-worth to their ability to please others. Saying no or setting boundaries might be perceived as a failure to meet this self-imposed standard, leading to guilt.
5. **Desire for Approval:** Humans naturally seek approval and acceptance from their social groups. Saying no may threaten this desire for approval, resulting in guilt.

It's important to recognize that setting boundaries is a healthy and necessary part of self-care and maintaining balanced relationships. Overcoming the feelings of guilt often involves practice, self-compassion, and a shift in perspective to understand that it's not selfish but essential for your well-being and for maintaining healthy relationships.

3 Practical Exercises – Firm Foundation of No

Develop the ability to say no and set boundaries effectively

1. **Create a Personal Bill of Rights:**
   - Exercise: Compile a list of your personal rights, such as "I have the right to say no," "I have the right to privacy," or "I have the right to be treated with respect."
   - Strategy: Having a personal bill of rights serves as a reminder of what you deserve in your interactions with others, aiding you in setting and protecting boundaries.

2. **Self-Awareness Exercise:**
   - Reflect on your values, needs, and limits. Make a list of what is most import-

ant to you in different areas of life, such as relationships, work, and personal well-being.
- Identify past situations where your boundaries were crossed, or you felt uncomfortable.
- This exercise helps you become more aware of your personal boundaries and what needs to be protected.

3. **The "No" Practice:**
   - Many people struggle with saying "no" when you need to set boundaries. In this exercise, practice saying "no" to low-stakes requests or situations.
   - You can start with small, inconsequential requests and gradually work on more significant ones. This helps build assertiveness and the ability to set boundaries effectively.

These strategies and exercises help you understand your boundaries, build assertiveness, and develop the skills needed to set and maintain healthy boundaries in different areas of your life.

"The Boundaries Foundation & Puff"

In Michelly's makeup bag, next to the supernatural cleansing wipe, lay a foundation that held a unique power, one that would help her set boundaries and learn to say "no" without guilt. It was no ordinary foundation; it had a glowing, complexion perfecting hue that seemed to shimmer with a hint of magic.

One day, as Michelly was preparing for a gathering with her friends, she couldn't shake the feeling of exhaustion that had been lingering for weeks. She had been overextending herself, constantly saying "yes" to everyone's requests, and as a result, her own well-being had taken a back seat. As she was getting ready for the event, she picked up the foundation, her fingers tingling with anticipation.

As Michelly applied the foundation, she noticed an unusual sensation. It felt as if the very act of applying the foundation was granting her the strength to set boundaries. A newfound confidence welled up within her, and she realized that this foundation held the power to help her assert herself.

At the gathering, when her friends began asking for more favors and additional commitments, Michelly felt the urge to say "yes" as she always had. But this time, she looked at herself in the mirror and remembered the boundaries she was learning to set. Her face matte sheen with the sheer magic; she mustered the courage to politely decline without guilt. She explained that she needed time for herself and that she couldn't take on any more right now.

Michelly's friends were taken aback at first, but as they saw the determination in her pores, they respected her decision. She realized that setting boundaries wasn't about being selfish; it was about self-care and self-preservation.

Over the following weeks, Michelly continued to use the foundation, both as a reminder of her newfound strength and as a symbol of her commitment to herself. With every press of puff, she felt more empowered to say "no" when necessary, without feeling guilty or anxious.

As the weeks turned into months, Michelly noticed a transformation in her life. She was no longer overburdened with commitments that drained her energy. Instead, she had time to focus on her own dreams and aspirations. The boundaries liner helped her navigate her personal and professional life with balance and confidence.

In time, Michelly found that her relationships had also improved. People respected her more for her honesty and appreciated the authenticity with which she communicated her boundaries. She felt more connected to those around her because she was no longer constantly overwhelmed and stressed.

The foundation and puff had become a symbol of empowerment and self-respect. It was a daily reminder that setting boundaries and saying "no" when needed was an essential part of self-care. Michelly had learned that it was not just about taking care of herself but also about nurturing the relationships that truly mattered. The power of the boundaries foundation & puff had transformed her life, allowing her to live more authentically and with a greater sense of inner peace.

"Each morning, as you line your eyes, let your inner vision be your guide to a day filled with positivity and radiance." MG

Line Your Eyes, Eyes Don't Lie:
Choosing Your Mood

Welcome to a chapter dedicated to helping you master the art of creating a positive mindset that ensures every day is a good day. Not so long ago, I witnessed a fascinating scene on my way to work when we were still commuting. A woman's outburst over getting cut off in traffic caught my attention, making me wonder how she'd let this minor hiccup ruin her day.

As she ranted and cursed, it seemed as though her world had crumbled. But in reality, all that happened was she was stuck at the red light while the other car made it through – an annoyance, not a catastrophe. Her dramatic reaction, honking her car's horn aggressively, made me question how long her day would be tainted by this incident.

This might not surprise you, as many of us react similarly. Negative experiences or interactions often dominate our thoughts and emotions for the entire day. This chapter will empower you to choose optimism, take control of your perspective, and determine the mood you want to maintain throughout your days. Did you know that choosing your mood is your choice? You decide who guides you every day, positivity or negativity.

1. **The Power of Optimism:** One of the most crucial decisions you can make is to become an optimist. Optimism involves being hopeful and confident about the future, expecting the best outcomes, and not dwelling on potential downsides. This doesn't mean you should ignore risks; it means focusing your energy on positive possibilities.
2. **A Positive Perspective:** Choosing a positive perspective involves deciding how

you want to see and experience life's events. It's about finding the silver lining in situations, even when things don't go as planned. Remember the lady with the parking ticket? She could have seen it as a lucky escape, not a disaster.

3. **Memory Management:** Learn to hold onto the good parts and archive the rest. Don't dwell on negative memories; extract wisdom and move forward. This approach doesn't mean forgetting unpleasant experiences but consciously deciding not to relive them. Make space for a happier mindset.

4. **Setting Your Intention:** Begin each day with a conscious choice to have a good day. Set a clear intention for how you want to feel and experience your day. Keep this intention in mind, especially when faced with challenges or hiccups.

5. **Conscious Choices Throughout the Day:** When faced with disruptions, remind yourself of your daily intention and consciously choose your responses. Avoid letting people or events derail your mood. Remember, you decide how situations impact you.

6. **No One Can Make You Unhappy:** Your happiness is your responsibility. Choose happiness as a way of life and make conscious decisions to support it. Life isn't something that merely happens to you; it's what you make of the events and experiences that come your way.

Life is a continuous series of moments, and by taking charge of your mindset, you can ensure that your days are filled with positivity and good moods. Remember, you have the power to determine how you experience each day. So, embrace optimism, choose your perspective, and keep your happiness in your own hands.

Our coaching session with Ashley, a mid-40s executive assistant, shed light on the profound impact that frustration had on her life and how Step Three, "Choose Your Mood," was a game-changer. Ashley expressed her newfound realization of the need to consciously choose happiness rather than just wishing for it. Here's what she had to say:

Ashley admitted that she often allowed frustration to overshadow her day. However, she had an epiphany during this step. By setting the intention to be happy, she could proactively reclaim her happiness, even in challenging situations. Ashley's real-life example of falling on her way to an Uber pickup and choosing happiness despite her embarrassment perfectly illustrated the power of choosing one's mood.

Now, let's recap the key takeaways from this chapter:

1. **Opt for Optimism:** Choose to be an optimist, remaining hopeful and confident about your future. Focus on the best possible outcomes without ignoring potential risks.
2. **Embrace a Positive Perspective:** Adopt a positive perspective, seeing life's events in the best light possible. Avoid allowing minor setbacks to turn into disasters.
3. **Memory Management:** Train your memory to remember the good parts of life and archive the rest. Learn from unpleasant experiences but choose not to dwell on them.
4. **Set Daily Intentions:** Start your day by setting a clear intention to have a good day.

This intention will guide your reactions and decisions as you navigate the day.
5. **Choose Your Thoughts:** Consciously choose your thoughts to generate the feelings you desire. Your thoughts have the power to shape your emotions.
6. **Take Responsibility for Your Happiness:** Recognize that your happiness is your responsibility. Commit to making happiness a way of life, not a distant goal.
7. **Determine How You Want to Feel:** Decide how you want to feel about your life. Life is what you make of the various experiences that come your way. You are in control of your responses and emotions.

As we move forward to Chapter Four, "Blush Honey Hush," we'll learn how to stop worrying about external judgments and opinions so that you can focus on making the most of your life without unnecessary distractions. Stay tuned for the next exciting chapter!

Make Up of the Brain –
Line Your Eyes, Eyes Don't Lie

Focusing more positively directly impacts your life and outcomes because it shapes your mindset, behavior, and interactions with others.

There are neurological and psychological mechanisms that can be triggered to make a person more positively influenced. Here are a few ways this can be achieved:

1. **Neuroplasticity:** The brain can rewire itself through neuroplasticity. Engaging in activities that promote positive thinking, such as mindfulness meditation or cognitive-behavioral therapy, can strengthen the neural pathways associated with positivity.
2. **Dopamine Release:** Engaging in rewarding and positive experiences, such as accomplishing goals, receiving praise, or experiencing acts of kindness, triggers the release of dopamine in the brain. This reinforces positive behavior and thinking.

3. **Gratitude Practice:** Regularly expressing gratitude and acknowledging positive aspects of life can activate the brain's reward center and enhance feelings of positivity.
4. **Social Connection:** Interactions with supportive and positive individuals can trigger the brain's social bonding and reward systems, leading to increased positivity.
5. **Positive Visualization:** Visualizing positive outcomes and experiences can activate the brain in ways that stimulate motivation and optimism.
6. **Exercise:** Physical activity, such as exercise, has been shown to release endorphins, which are natural mood lifters that promote positivity.
7. **Adequate Sleep:** Ensuring good sleep habits can contribute to a balanced emotional state and a more positive outlook.

By engaging in activities and practices that target these brain mechanisms, individuals can become more positively influenced and experience a greater sense of positivity in their lives.

3 Practical Exercises – Line the Eyes, Eyes Don't Lie

Positively influence their mood each day

1. **Gratitude Journaling:**
   - Keep a gratitude journal. Every day, write down three things you're grateful for. These can be small or significant aspects of your life.
   - Reflect on why these things make you feel thankful and how they contribute to your well-being.
   - This exercise helps shift your focus toward positive aspects of life, fostering a more optimistic and contented mood.

2. **Positive Affirmations:**
   - Create a list of positive affirmations. These are short, uplifting statements that challenge negative self-talk and promote self-empowerment.
   - Recite these affirmations daily, especially in the morning, to start the day with a positive mindset.

- Repeated use of affirmations can gradually alter thought patterns, boosting self-confidence and positivity.

3. **Visualization Exercise:**
    - Guide yourself through a daily visualization exercise where you imagine a positive outcome or a desired mood for the day.
    - Picture this scenario in detail, including how you would feel, what you would see, and what you would do.
    - This exercise helps set a positive tone for the day and can boost motivation and mood.

These exercises provide practical and effective ways to influence your mood positively daily. Remind yourself that consistency and patience are key to experiencing long-term benefits.

"The Mood Mastery Liner"

Within Michelly's makeup bag, alongside the enchanting cleansing wipe and the empowering boundaries liner, there was a unique eyeliner with a transformative power. This eyeliner, known as the "Mood Mastery Liner," held the secret to mastering one's mood and choosing positivity every day.

Michelly had always been prone to mood swings. Some days she would wake up full of energy and optimism, while on other days, she struggled to find a hint of positivity. She longed for a more stable and positive emotional state.

One morning, Michelly decided to use the Mood Mastery Liner as she got ready for the day. As she carefully applied the eyeliner, she felt a soothing, calming sensation. The deep emerald-green hue seemed to emanate a tranquil energy, and she sensed that it held the power to influence her mood.

Throughout the day, Michelly carried a small mirror in her bag, allowing her to glimpse at her eyes lined with the Mood Mastery Liner. She realized that the eyeliner had an astonishing effect on her emotions. Whenever she felt her mood slipping into negativity, she would look into the mirror and see the emerald lines. The liner served as a reminder to pause, take a deep breath, and choose a positive perspective.

Over time, Michelly learned to master her mood and cultivate a more positive outlook. The Mood Mastery Liner encouraged her to become more mindful of her emotions and reactions. She discovered that even in challenging situations, she could choose positivity. With a simple glance at her lined eyes, she found the strength to control her emotional response.

Michelly's transformation didn't happen overnight, but the Mood Mastery Liner was a valuable tool in her journey. It taught her that her mood was within her control, and she had the power to decide how she wanted to feel each day.

As days turned into weeks and weeks into months, Michelly noticed a profound shift in her life. She experienced greater resilience in the face of adver-

sity, improved relationships with others, and a heightened sense of well-being. Choosing positivity became a way of life, and she realized that she was no longer a victim of her own irritability.

The Mood Mastery Liner had taught her that mastering one's mood wasn't about suppressing negative emotions but about acknowledging them and consciously choosing a positive response. Michelly found that this eyeliner was not just a cosmetic but a daily source of inspiration and empowerment.

In the end, Michelly understood that the power of the Mood Mastery Liner lay in her own mind and heart. The eyeliner was a catalyst, a tangible reminder that she could influence her mood and choose positivity every day. It had helped her unlock a profound sense of inner peace and emotional well-being, transforming her life into a more joyful and fulfilling experience.

"Silence your inner critic, for within you lay a wellspring of self-confidence waiting to be heard." MG

Blush Honey Hush:

Ignoring Negativity and Embracing Fear

In this chapter, we're going to embark on a journey, much like my mother did when she got ready, adding that perfect touch of blush to her cheeks, a dash of confidence that lit up the room. It's all about silencing the relentless inner and outer voices that threaten to dim your light.

You see, it's vital not only to rein in your inner critic but also to shield yourself from external critics.

Letting others' opinions, well-intentioned or malevolent, shape your path is like running a race but never leaving the starting line. It's a disservice to your potential and your dreams. Let's explore how to transform your perception of negative feedback, criticism, and backhanded compliments.

I'll share a valuable strategy I use to decipher whose feedback truly matters to me. My mentor once offered profound wisdom: "Some will, some won't. So, what?" This message, simple yet impactful, reminds us that opinions about us, be they good or bad, don't define our worth. You must question why it should matter so much. Why prioritize others' opinions over your own?

Here's the first critical mindset shift: Realize that when someone judges you or offers criticism, it's about them, not you. Their thoughts, values, and ideals shape their judgment, not your essence. It might feel uncomfortable, but their opinion is theirs alone.

As a coach, I emphasize "no thoughts, no feelings, no values, no judgments" when training others. In this role, your responsibility is to listen, not impose your agenda or standards. This mindset can protect you from external judgments.

Remember, you're not obliged to accept someone's opinion, no matter how it's presented. It's just that – an opinion. Once you differentiate opinions from facts, it becomes easier to let negative feedback slide right off you. Imagine it as criticisms rolling off a non-stick pan – effortlessly.

But this mindset isn't enough if you continue to be your own harshest critic. You must shift your internal self-talk. Become your own biggest fan, offering yourself unwavering support and encouragement, regardless of outcomes.

Also, remember that opinions aren't facts. Most of the time, you're receiving someone's perspective, not an absolute truth. This realization can empower you to let negative opinions go, lifting a significant weight from your shoulders.

When choosing whose opinion matters, create an inner circle of trusted individuals who understand your values and unconditionally support you. But even then, you're not obligated to accept their opinions. Listening is enough.

Above all, recognize that your self-belief shouldn't rely on others' opinions. Your self-esteem should be independent of external judgments. If it's based on external validation, your self-worth will crumble when things don't go your way.

Lastly, never speak to yourself more harshly than you would to a small child. You are the guardian of your self-esteem. Treat yourself with the kindness and encouragement you deserve.

As you progress through this chapter, I hope you'll leave with a newfound strength to ignore the noise and continue your journey with confidence and self-assurance. Remember, you are your own greatest champion.

In this chapter, we've taken a journey through the power of silencing the critical voices, both internal and external, that hold you back. I had the privilege of speaking with Naomi, a 54-year-old Life Coach & Health Mentor, who shared her incredible transformation through Step Four – Blush Honey Hush.

Naomi candidly acknowledged that while she liked to believe she didn't care about others' opinions, the truth was different. Childhood experiences of being picked on for her weight and size had left their mark on her confidence. But Step Four became a revelation for her, highlighting how she clung to these experiences and the need for a profound mindset shift.

The key insight Naomi gained was recognizing the difference between wanting people to like her and needing it. Through this chapter, she learned to release the shackles of others' criticisms, realizing that these judgments are often projections of their own fears and beliefs. It's about them, not you.

Naomi concluded that seeking acceptance and approval is energy-consuming work, and she doesn't need to put so much importance on it. She decided to be her own cheerleader and only sought advice from those she truly trusted, knowing that she alone was responsible for how she felt about herself.

Self-doubt, one of the most relentless voices, was something Naomi vowed to silence. She committed to being her own compass and following her inner calling, which led her to pursue her dream of starting a YouTube channel, despite her past hesitations.

Now, let's recap the most important takeaways from Step Four:

1. Realize that judgments and criticism from others are reflections of their own concerns, not your worth.
2. Remember that opinions are just opinions, not facts, regardless of how they're presented.
3. Develop emotional Teflon to let criticism and negative opinions slide right off.
4. Stop worrying about what others think and don't let the fear of judgment hinder your progress.
5. Choose a trusted inner circle of cheerleaders whose opinions genuinely matter.
6. Become your most fervent supporter, as the most crucial opinion is your own.
7. Treat yourself with kindness and guard your self-esteem wisely.

In the next chapter, Step Five: Confront the Enemy, we'll dive into how to tackle your fears and conquer the obstacles that have held you back. Get ready to unlock your full potential and become the master of your destiny.

Make Up of the Brain – Blush Honey Hush

Self-doubt and the inner critic hurt people by undermining their confidence and well-being. When you doubt yourself or engage in self-critical thinking, it can lead to:

1. **Lower Self-Esteem:** Self-doubt and criticism erode your sense of self-worth, making you feel less capable and valuable.
2. **Reduced Motivation:** Negative self-talk can diminish your motivation to pursue goals and take on challenges.
3. **Increased Anxiety:** Constant self-doubt can lead to anxiety and stress, affecting your mental and emotional health.
4. **Missed Opportunities:** It can prevent you from seizing opportunities and trying new things, limiting personal and professional growth.
5. **Strained Relationships:** Self-doubt can lead to insecurity, affecting how you inter-

act with others and potentially straining relationships.
6. **Unfulfilled Potential:** When you doubt yourself, you may not realize your full potential and miss out on opportunities for success and happiness.

Overcoming self-doubt and silencing the inner critic is essential for personal growth, improved mental health, and achieving your goals. It allows you to tap into your true potential and live a more fulfilling life.

Self-doubt often has its roots in both psychological and neurological factors. Some of the neurological and psychological mechanisms that can contribute to self-doubt include:

1. **Negative Bias:** The brain has a natural tendency to pay more attention to negative information as a survival mechanism. This can lead to a focus on one's weaknesses or past failures, fueling self-doubt.
2. **Fear of Rejection:** The brain's social processing areas are highly developed, and fear of social rejection can lead to self-doubt. The brain places a high value on

social belonging, making the fear of not fitting in or being accepted a potent source of self-doubt.
3. **Inner Critic:** The brain's prefrontal cortex is responsible for self-monitoring and self-reflection. It can create an "inner critic" that analyzes and evaluates one's actions, often leading to self-criticism and self-doubt.
4. **Past Experiences:** Negative past experiences, especially in childhood, can shape the brain's perception of one's capabilities and contribute to self-doubt.
5. **Social Comparison:** People tend to compare themselves to others, and this can lead to self-doubt if you perceive themselves as falling short in comparison.
6. **Neurotransmitters:** Imbalances in neurotransmitters like serotonin and dopamine can influence mood and self-esteem, potentially contributing to self-doubt.

It's important to recognize that self-doubt is a common human experience, but it can be managed and even overcome through techniques like cognitive-behavioral therapy, mindfulness, and self-compassion practices. These approaches can help individuals reframe their thoughts and beliefs to reduce self-doubt and enhance self-confidence.

3 Practical Exercises – Blush Honey Hush

Removing Self Doubt & Silencing the Inner Critic

1. **Challenge Negative Self-Talk:**
   - Pay attention to your self-talk and identify self-doubt triggers. This might include phrases like "I can't," "I'm not good enough," or "I always mess things up."
   - Challenge these negative thoughts by asking for evidence and considering more balanced perspectives. Often, self-doubt is based on unfounded beliefs.

2. **Set Achievable Goals:**
   - Break down your goals into smaller, more achievable steps. Setting realistic goals and achieving them gradually can boost confidence and reduce self-doubt.

- Celebrate each small success to reinforce the belief that you can reach your larger goals.

3. **Practice Self-Compassion:**
   - Emphasize the importance of self-compassion. Treat yourself with the same kindness and understanding you would offer to a friend facing self-doubt.
   - Remind yourself that everyone makes mistakes and faces challenges, and self-compassion can help you navigate self-doubt with greater resilience.

By implementing these practical tips, you can work on reducing self-doubt and building a stronger sense of self-confidence over time. Remember to seek out a good coach to provide ongoing support and guidance as you make progress in this area. If you don't have one, reach out to me and my team to connect you one at michellegines.online.

"The Self-Worth Blush: Honey Hush"

Inside Michelly's makeup bag, amidst the supernatural cleansing wipe, the empowering boundaries foundation & puff, and the mood mastery liner, there was a remarkable blush with a name that piqued her curiosity: "Honey Hush." Little did she know that this blush held the secret to unpacking the notion of ignoring negativity and focusing on self-worth.

Michelly had always been sensitive to criticism and negativity, often allowing the words and opinions of others to affect her self-esteem. She yearned for a way to rise above the negativity that seemed to cloud her thoughts and chip away at her self-worth.

One morning, while getting ready for work, Michelly decided to try the Honey Hush blush. As she applied it to her cheeks, she felt an immediate warmth and a gentle, reassuring presence. The blush had a radiant, golden hue, and as she looked at herself in the mirror, she sensed it had the power to help her unpack the notion of ignoring negativity.

Throughout the day, Michelly faced various instances of negativity, both from others and from her own inner critic. Instead of letting these remarks and self-doubt fester, she thought of the Honey Hush blush. It seemed to whisper in her ear, encouraging her to silence the negativity with a touch of self-worth.

Michelly began to visualize the golden blush acting as a protective shield against negativity. Every time she felt hurt or devalued, she mentally applied a layer of Honey Hush to her self-esteem. The blush served as a reminder that her worth was not determined by the judgments of others or her own insecurities.

Over time, Michelly's perspective on negativity transformed. She no longer allowed it to define her self-worth. She recognized that ignoring negativity didn't mean disregarding constructive criticism but rather refusing to internalize harmful words or let them erode her confidence.

As days turned into weeks and weeks into months, Michelly's self-worth blossomed like a radiant blush on her cheeks. She found that she had become more resilient, self-assured, and immune to the influences of negative people and thoughts. The Honey Hush blush was a daily affirmation of her inherent value, and it had become her secret ally in the pursuit of self-worth.

Michelly learned that she could choose to focus on her strengths, talents, and the love and respect she had for herself. She understood that self-worth was not a fleeting emotion but a steadfast foundation upon which she could build a more fulfilling and positive life.

In the end, the Honey Hush blush was a metaphorical and tangible representation of her commitment to prioritizing self-worth over negativity. It was a reminder that her value was inherent and not contingent on the judgments of others or her own self-critique. Michelly had found the key to unpacking the notion of ignoring negativity and embracing her self-worth, allowing her to live a more empowered and fulfilling life.

"Like long-lasting mascara that endures through challenges, eliminating self-sabotage strengthens your resilience and beauty, revealing the enduring power within." MG

Mind Your Mount Mascara:
Embracing Fear and Conquering Self-Sabotage

Fear – it's a word that can send shivers down our spines, and it's often the barrier that stands between us and our dreams. But fear doesn't have to be the enemy. In fact, by the end of this chapter, you'll have a new perspective on how fear can be a driving force in your life, and you'll know exactly how to use it to your advantage.

Fear is a natural part of life, something that many people often misunderstand and try to avoid. Let's get one thing straight – I'm not talking about those common fears like spiders, heights, or things that go bump in the night. The fears we're discussing here run much deeper. These fears reside in the very core of your being, ready to erode your self-confidence and self-belief if you let them. But guess what? You don't have to hide from these fears because they aren't harbingers of doom. In fact, they often signal something profoundly important.

So, let's start with a fundamental shift in mindset – fear is your subconscious way of telling you that something matters. As someone often labeled as fearless, I can tell you, I'm not actually fearless. Instead, I operate under the motto of "allow fear to stop me less often." I've become skilled at confronting and disempowering my fears over the years, but it wasn't until I faced a lifelong dream that I truly grasped the nature of fear.

In my teenage years, I aspired to be an actor, or more precisely, a movie star. But I had been told I wasn't fit for the screen due to my crooked teeth and some other insecurities. So, I settled for a career as a news writer. However, that longing to be in front of the camera lingered deep within me. It was my nagging "what if" – what if I'd chosen the wrong path, what if I was missing my calling? This feeling haunted me, sometimes quietly and at other times loudly.

At 25, I found myself in a situation with two job opportunities. One involved leading a team for a greeting card company during a national rebranding, and the other required me to move away from home to work in sales for a telecommunications startup. It was a leap into the unknown, and the fear that I wasn't qualified enough crept in. But I decided to take the leap, adopting the "fake it 'til you make it" approach.

I dressed in my best power suit and entered the first interview, feeling a mix of excitement and fear. The closer I got, the more my excitement turned to nervousness. The fear I felt wasn't specific; it wasn't about forgetting lines or impressing the interviewers. It ran much deeper. I recognized that this was my chance to follow my dreams. This interview could change everything for me. I realized the true importance of the situation. And that's what fear was trying to convey – these matters in a way, nothing in my career had ever mattered before.

The second interview went well too, but as I drove home, I had a moment of clarity. Sales might not be my true calling. The thought of selling phone services day in and day out didn't resonate with me. Despite receiving job offers from both interviews, I chose the role of Installation Supervisor with the greeting card company. This job turned out to be a dream come true, with opportunities to travel and explore the country.

Eventually, I was promoted to a sales position, living my dream, even if it took a different path than I had initially imagined. If I hadn't faced that initial interview, I would have never discovered this. If I had interpreted my fear as a sign that the program wasn't right for me, I would have missed a life-changing opportunity. Don't give your fears more power than they deserve. Fear often serves as a sign that something is important to you. Listen to it carefully.

The next step in conquering fear is understanding where it comes from. Fear of failure is a common culprit that holds people back. But fear of success is just as destructive. Success can bring change, busyness, and responsibilities that you might be unprepared for. It's vital to recognize these fears and address them, as they can lead to self-sabotage.

On the flip side, fear of disrupting the status quo can also hold you back. You might be worried that pursuing your goals will compromise the things that currently work in your life. Balancing the pursuit of your dreams and the things you value is essential.

Lastly, make friends with your fears. Get to know them, understand them, and use them as guides rather than adversaries. Fear doesn't have to be a barrier; it can be a driving force. Use affirmations to change your mindset and reshape your relationship with fear. Acknowledge your fears, learn from them, and carry on.

Remember, fear is a part of life, but allowing it to stand in your way is a choice. Make the choice to confront your fears and move forward. It's not about conquering them; it's about understanding and accepting them. By doing so, you empower yourself to navigate the challenges and uncertainties of life with confidence and determination.

In today's coaching session, we've seen firsthand how confronting our fears and embracing them can lead to transformative insights. Candy, a 35-year-old nurse practitioner, shared her journey towards understanding and overcoming her fear of failure, specifically in the context of her long-distance hiking aspirations.

Candy's candid reflection highlighted some fundamental takeaways from this chapter:

1. **Fear Signals Importance:** Fear is a natural part of life, a signal from our subconscious that something truly matters. It's a sign that we care deeply about the outcome.
2. **Don't Over-Empower Your Fears:** We should never give our fears more power than they deserve. They're not all-consuming monsters, but rather messengers, letting us know that we're on a significant path.
3. **No Need for Battle:** The key is not to go into battle with your fears. You don't have to conquer them or suppress them before moving forward. Acknowledge them and carry on.

4. **Fear Isn't a Roadblock:** You don't need to let your fears stand in your way. Even though you feel fear, it doesn't mean you have to alter your course or choose a different path.
5. **Understanding the Source:** Taking time to understand the real source of your fears is crucial. Avoid a life lived in fear; confront your fears and use them as guides to important discoveries.
6. **Fear of Disrupting the Status Quo:** Don't let the fear of disrupting the status quo hold you back from making essential changes in your life. It's all about balance and understanding what truly matters to you.
7. **Befriending Your Fears:** Lastly, become friends with your fears. Get to know them, understand them, and use them as companions on your journey. Don't judge them; instead, look for the valuable lessons they offer.

As we move into the next chapter, Step 6, you'll learn how to bid farewell to one of the most common roadblocks – the infamous "But." We'll show you how to get out of your own way and stop allowing your mouth to be a big obstacle to your success. So, get ready for a Lipstick Shift that will ensure your lips don't lie.

Make Up of Your Brain –
Mind Your Mount Mascara

Self-sabotage hinders and hurts people by causing them to act against their own best interests or goals. It typically involves behaviors, thoughts, or habits that undermine their well-being and success. Here's how self-sabotage can be harmful:

1. **Prevents Progress:** Self-sabotage often leads to procrastination, avoidance, or making choices that hinder progress and prevent individuals from reaching their goals.
2. **Undermines Confidence:** Engaging in self-sabotaging behaviors can erode self-confidence and self-esteem, leading to doubt and negative self-talk.
3. **Increases Stress:** Self-sabotage can create stress and anxiety as individuals recognize

that their own actions or choices are causing setbacks.
4. **Limits Opportunities:** By sabotaging their efforts, individuals miss out on opportunities for personal and professional growth and success.
5. **Strains Relationships:** Self-sabotage can also affect relationships, as it may lead to unmet commitments, disappointments, or conflicts with others.

Self-sabotage can hinder personal growth, undermine confidence, increase stress, limit opportunities, and strain relationships, ultimately impeding individuals from achieving their full potential and living a fulfilling life.

As we've seen in other areas self-sabotage often has roots in psychological and cognitive factors, and there is no specific brain mechanism that triggers self-sabotage. However, several cognitive and emotional processes may contribute to self-sabotaging behaviors, including:

1. **Fear of Failure:** The brain's amygdala, responsible for processing emotions like

fear, can trigger self-sabotage when individuals are afraid of failing or facing potential criticism or rejection.

2. **Negative Self-Beliefs:** The brain's prefrontal cortex plays a role in self-monitoring and self-reflection. Negative self-beliefs can lead to self-sabotaging behaviors by fueling self-doubt and a lack of self-worth.

3. **Procrastination:** The brain's prefrontal cortex can become overwhelmed when confronted with complex tasks. This can lead to procrastination and self-sabotage, as individuals delay acting on important goals.

4. **Habitual Behavior:** The brain's basal ganglia reinforce habitual behaviors. If self-sabotaging actions have become routine, the brain can perpetuate these behaviors.

5. **Stress and Coping Mechanisms:** High levels of stress can trigger self-sabotage as individuals' resort to maladaptive coping mechanisms, such as overeating or substance abuse, to manage stress.

While the brain doesn't directly cause self-sabotage, understanding these cognitive and emotional factors is important for addressing and overcoming self-sabotaging behaviors. Techniques like cognitive-behavioral therapy, mindfulness, and self-awareness can help individuals manage and reduce self-sabotage.

3 Practical Exercises – Mind Your Mount Mascara

Overcome self-sabotage in various areas of Your Life

1. **Identify Triggers and Patterns:**
   - **Exercise:** Keep a journal where they document instances of self-sabotage. Note what they were thinking, feeling, and doing leading up to the self-sabotaging behavior.
   - **Strategy:** This exercise helps you identify common triggers and patterns that lead to self-sabotage. Once you recognize these triggers, you can work on developing strategies to avoid or cope with them differently.

2. **Develop a Self-Compassion Practice:**
   - **Exercise:** Practice self-compassion by writing a self-compassion letter. In this exercise, you write a letter to yourself as if you were writing to a friend who was going through a similar self-sabotaging situation.
   - **Strategy:** Self-compassion helps you be kinder to yourself and reduce negative self-talk that can lead to self-sabotage. This exercise fosters a sense of understanding and self-support.

3. **Set Specific Goals and Action Plans:**
   - **Exercise:** Assist yourself in setting clear, specific goals in the areas where you tend to self-sabotage. Break down these goals into smaller, manageable steps and create action plans for achieving them.
   - **Strategy:** By setting well-defined goals and creating actionable steps, you have a clear roadmap for progress. This can reduce feelings of overwhelm and procrastination, mitigating self-sabotaging behaviors.

These strategies and exercises can empower you to understand and address self-sabotage in your life, leading to more positive and constructive behaviors that align with your goals and aspirations. Remember to provide ongoing support and guidance as they work through these challenges.

"The 'Mind Your Mount' Mascara"

In Michelly's makeup bag, among the collection of transformative beauty products, there was a mascara with a name that piqued her interest: "Mind Your Mount." Little did she know that this mascara held the power to help her understand and overcome the self-sabotage that had hindered her success and happiness. The truth was told when Breanna West said, 'The Mountain is You'.

Michelly had always been ambitious, but it seemed that whenever she was close to achieving her dreams, self-sabotage crept in. She questioned her own worth, allowed doubts to fester, and found herself pulling back just when she should have been charging forward.

One day, as Michelly prepared for a crucial job interview, she decided to try the "Mind Your Mount" mascara. It had a deep, inky-black shade that felt like a suit of armor for her lashes. As she carefully applied it, she noticed an intriguing sensation. It was as though the mascara had connected her to a wellspring of inner strength and self-awareness.

Throughout the interview, Michelly couldn't help but think about the mascara. It reminded her to be mindful of her own thoughts and behaviors. It was like a little voice whispering in her ear, "Mind your mount," reminding her not to self-sabotage.

Over the following weeks, Michelly began to pay close attention to her self-sabotaging tendencies. She noticed the moments when she hesitated to speak up, fearing her own inadequacy. She observed her inclination to downplay her achievements or undermine her worth. With "Mind Your Mount" mascara framing her eyes, she became more self-aware and recognized the patterns that had been holding her back.

As she delved deeper into the complexities of self-sabotage, Michelly made a commitment to face her fears and doubts head-on. Every time she felt the urge to retreat or undermine her potential, she visualized the mascara as her mount, the embodiment of her inner strength and resolve.

With time, Michelly found herself mastering the art of "minding her mount." She no longer allowed self-sabotage to hinder her path to success and happiness. The mascara served as a constant reminder that she was in control of her destiny, and her doubts should never be the rider of her journey.

As weeks turned into months, Michelly's life began to transform. She achieved successes she had previously thought were unattainable. Her relationships flourished, her confidence soared, and her happiness knew no bounds. The "Mind Your Mount" mascara was her silent companion in this journey, a symbol of her ability to overcome self-sabotage.

In the end, the "Mind Your Mount" mascara was not just a cosmetic wand, but a powerful tool that taught her to be mindful of her self-sabotaging tendencies and to trust in her own worth. She learned that self-sabotage was not an insurmountable obstacle, but rather a challenge to be met head-on. Michelly had found the key to managing self-sabotage and, in doing so, unlocked the doors to a life filled with success and happiness.

"Let your lips shift from excuses to affirmations and watch your life transform." MG

Lipstick Shift:
Bidding Farewell to Reasons and Excuses

Welcome to Step Six – Time for a Lipstick Shift. Really, I wanted to call this chapter, your but is too big. However, to tie in with the makeup bag I had to go this way because the way we deal with this but is with our mouth. So, you see how the message fits, so keep following along. Now, don't worry, you're not in the wrong place; this isn't a sudden shift to a dieting book. Although, like many women, there are days when I wish I could say goodbye to my "butt" (as in the extra weight around the derrière). Again, that's not the "but" we're discussing in this chapter. The "but" I'm talking about is the one with a single 'T' – the one that precedes all your excuses.

The biggest obstacle in most people's way is, well, themselves. They make promises they know they'll never keep and set goals that are nearly impossible to achieve. They list endless excuses for what they haven't done and then wonder why their confidence dwindles. Most people can rattle off a long list of reasons why their life isn't all it could be.

The truth is, they're their own worst enemy, sabotaging their own success by overpromising and under-delivering. They set goals they don't believe they can achieve or even deserve to achieve. Perfectionism, although a nice concept, is an impossible aim. Most people have areas in their lives where they could make significant improvements if only, they'd get out of their own way. If they faced their fears, overcame their limiting beliefs, managed their resources better, and were honest about time management, they could stop making excuses and start being accountable to themselves.

First things first, let's stop undermining your self-confidence by providing a "get out" clause even before you begin. Have you ever caught yourself thinking about something you need or want to do, and simultaneously formulating the excuse you'll give for not doing it, before you even get started? It may sound crazy when spelled out like this, but it's surprisingly common. I've been guilty of it too. In the past week alone, you can probably recall an instance where you committed to doing something, only to immediately follow it up with a "but" and an excuse.

Each time you utter that dreaded "but" you're essentially giving yourself a preemptive excuse to fail. More significantly, you're undermining your self-belief. What you're telling yourself is, "I never really believed I could do it. I don't think I can do it. Or it doesn't matter if I do it." As Yoda wisely said, "Do or do not, there is no try."

Your next mindset shift is to own your choices instead of making excuses. Everything in life comes down to choices. You consciously and subconsciously make choices throughout your day, determining whether you'll hit snooze, attend your meeting early, or exercise after a long day. The realization that even seemingly insignificant choices are continually guiding your life can help you navigate your day more effectively and keep it on track.

You should be aware that not all choices have a clear right or wrong answer, and some choices are essential to your life's success. If a choice propels you forward, then it's the right one. The goal is to take actions aligned with your intentions and values, ones that will move you closer to your vision of the future.

Sometimes, finding motivation can be elusive. You might feel stuck or unmotivated to pursue your goals. If you've ever found yourself in this position, you need to explore what's really holding you back. Remember, people do what works. If something isn't working in one area of your life, it's because it's working for you in some other way. Identify these silent beliefs or benefits that hinder your progress and adjust them.

So, you've stopped making excuses and started owning your choices, but you're still struggling to stick to your commitments. This may be because your goals and targets are unrealistic. Setting achievable goals is key to staying motivated. If you revisit your goals and find that they are no longer suitable, delete them.

Large, audacious goals can be inspiring, but more often, they set you up for failure. Your mission should be to improve your life by 10% in each area you want to change. This small, manageable shift will serve as your starting point. Once you've mastered this 10% improvement, you can reassess your goals. Small steps can lead to significant results, so don't feel pressured to tackle everything all at once.

Now, let's not forget that self-belief is the secret sauce to your success. If you want to shift your mindset away from excuses and towards meeting your commitments with ease, you may also need to adjust the way you think about yourself. Self-belief and commitment are crucial in accomplishing your goals. Remember, your beliefs about your own capacity can greatly affect your self-discipline. You should not anchor your self-belief on past experiences or lack of them; shift your self-talk to something more future-focused.

So, say goodbye to your "but," and let go of the excuses that have been holding you back. Embrace self-belief, make smarter commitments, and create lasting change by starting with a 10% improvement. Your life is full of choices; make the ones that propel you towards your vision for the future. With the right mindset, you'll find it easier to accomplish your commitments and goals and ultimately leave excuses behind.

Welcome to the conclusion of Step Six, "Say Goodbye to Your 'But'". We had the chance to speak with Mary, a blogger in her early 30s, and her insights from this chapter are truly enlightening.

Step Six resonated with Mary on a deeply personal level. She confessed to being an analytical person, someone who has spent her career meticulously finding defects and reasons not to release products. Unfortunately, this tendency for perfectionism also extends to her own life and goals. She shared how she could talk herself out of nearly anything – exercise, dieting, working on personal projects, even having fun. The cycle of excuses left her feeling miserable.

Mary talked about the familiar pattern of joining a gym, setting unrealistic expectations, and then feeling like a failure when she didn't meet those expectations. It was a costly cycle, both in terms of money and self-esteem. But now, she's realized the power of starting with a 10% improvement rather than an all-

or-nothing approach. Enthusiasm doesn't equal true motivation, and she's decided to let go of the past as a definition of who she is. No more excuses, she declares.

Let's recap the key lessons from Step Six:

1. **Do It or Don't Do It:** Don't give yourself an excuse to fail before you even begin. Say goodbye to "try."
2. **Own Your Choices:** Instead of making excuses, consciously make choices that align with your values and intentions.
3. **People Do What Works:** If you're not making consistent progress, find your missing motivation.
4. **Values as Motivation:** Your values can be a powerful source of motivation. Let them guide you.
5. **Commit to What You Really Want:** By committing only to things that align with your values, you'll find it easy to leave excuses behind.
6. **Small Steps to Big Leaps:** Start with a 10% shift. Small steps can lead to significant change.

7. **Nurture Self-Belief:** Your self-belief is the secret sauce to success. Believe in yourself and your abilities.

With these powerful insights, you're now ready for Step Seven: "See into the Future." In the next chapter, we'll show you how to shift your focus to what you truly want in life by understanding your values and setting clear intentions for your future. It's time for a fresh face to the future!

Make Up of the Brain – Lipstick Shift

There are cognitive and neurological factors that contribute to people making up excuses and reasons for not acting or holding themselves accountable. Some of these factors include:

1. **Cognitive Dissonance:** The brain seeks to maintain cognitive consistency, and when actions or beliefs conflict, it can lead to discomfort. To reduce this discomfort, people may make up excuses to justify their actions or inaction.
2. **Fear of Failure:** The brain's amygdala, responsible for processing emotions, can

trigger fear responses when faced with the possibility of failure. This fear may lead individuals to make excuses to avoid acting and facing potential failure.
3. **Procrastination:** The brain's prefrontal cortex, responsible for executive functions like decision-making and impulse control, can become overwhelmed when faced with a task. This can lead to procrastination, with excuses used to justify delays.
4. **Confirmation Bias:** The brain tends to favor information that confirms existing beliefs. People may make up excuses to support their current beliefs and actions, even if they are counterproductive.
5. **Social Influence:** Human brains are highly attuned to social dynamics. People may make excuses to align with social norms, gain approval, or avoid social disapproval.

Recognizing these cognitive and emotional factors is a crucial step in addressing the tendency to make excuses. By understanding how the brain works, individuals can work on improving accountability, reducing procrastination, and making more informed decisions. Techniques like cognitive-behavioral therapy and mindfulness can be helpful in managing these cognitive processes.

3 Practical Exercises – Lipstick Shift

Overcome the habit of making up excuses and reasons for not taking action.

1. **Accountability Journaling:**
   - Keep an "Accountability Journal." In this journal, you should document your goals, the actions you need to take, and any excuses or reasons that come to mind for not taking action.
   - Reflect on each excuse and explore whether it's valid or simply a rationalization to avoid action.
   - Challenge yourself to come up with alternative, action-oriented responses to counteract you excuses.

2. **The "5 Whys" Technique:**
   - Utilize the "5 Whys" technique. When you catch yourself making excuses, ask yourself to repeatedly ask "Why?" to

dig deeper into the root cause of your resistance.
- By exploring the underlying motivations and fears, you can gain insight into your behavior and work on addressing the real issues holding them back.

3. **Visualize Success:**
   - Embrace Visualization. With a strong visualization exercise, you vividly imagine the successful completion of a task, a real win or achieving a goal.
   - Incorporate positive emotions and sensations associated with this success and to feel like it's already done.
   - Regularly practicing this exercise can boost motivation and reduce the tendency to make excuses.

These exercises will help you become more self-aware, challenge your excuses, and develop strategies for acting. Over time, you can break the habit of making up reasons to avoid responsibility and achieve your goals.

"The 'Lipstick Shift'"

Inside Michelly's makeup bag, along with the other transformative beauty products, there was a lipstick with an intriguing name: "The Lipstick Shift." Little did she know that this lipstick held the key to eliminating excuses and reasons that had been holding her back from achieving her goals.

Michelly had always dreamed of pursuing her passion for writing but constantly found herself making excuses to delay or avoid it altogether. She blamed a lack of time, her busy schedule, and her inner doubts for not taking the leap.

One day, as she prepared for another day at her uninspiring office job, she decided to try "The Lipstick Shift." It was a bold, vibrant red that seemed to radiate determination. As she applied the lipstick, she noticed a subtle change in her demeanor. It was as though the lipstick had emboldened her to take charge of her dreams.

Throughout the day, Michelly felt a newfound confidence coursing through her veins. She no longer used her old excuses to justify her inaction. The lipstick was her reminder that she had the power to eliminate the excuses that held her back.

In the following weeks, Michelly began to scrutinize her self-imposed limitations. She realized that her excuses were mere roadblocks to her dreams. With "The Lipstick Shift" now her signature shade, she found herself addressing these excuses head-on.

Whenever the thought of not having enough time or fearing failure crept into her mind, she'd reach for the lipstick and apply it as if it were armor. It was her symbol of determination, her way of shifting her mindset and her mouth away from excuses.

With time, Michelly saw remarkable changes in her life. She was no longer held back by reasons that seemed trivial in the grand scheme of her dreams. The lipstick had become a symbol of her commitment to her own success and her determination to eliminate excuses. The words she used were now more pivotal than ever in guiding and propelling her path forward.

As months turned into a year, Michelly took a leap of faith and started her writing and speaking journey. She no longer lets excuses deter her from her goals. She was writing, submitting her work, and making progress toward her dream. "The Lipstick Shift" had empowered her to transform her life, to act, and to pursue her passion.

In the end, "The Lipstick Shift" wasn't just words but a voice teaching the significance of eliminating excuses and reasons that held herself or others back. She understood that excuses are self-imposed limitations, and with the right mindset and determination, could be overcome. Michelly had found the key to taking charge of her dreams, and in doing so, she'd unlocked the doors to a future filled with purpose and fulfillment and now teaching others the same.

"Embrace a fresh face forward, and dive into the boundless power of setting your intentions and goals, for within them lies the path to your dreams." MG

Mirror a Fresh Face Forward:
Setting Clear Intentions for Your Life

Welcome to the exhilarating finale of the seven-step journey in "Girl, Make Up Your Mind"! Congratulations on reaching this milestone. We've covered a lot of ground together, and I'm thrilled about the mindset shifts you've made and the exciting transformations that await you.

In this concluding chapter, we'll cast our gaze toward the future and harness the power of your newfound mindset. We'll explore what you should focus on and what to let go of to turn your dream life into a vibrant reality. I'll also share why it's crucial not to view your goals as the ultimate destination and where to direct your attention instead. Often, people spend more time planning their vacation than planning their lives. But remember, the life you truly desire won't simply materialize; you must define, design, and plan it to ensure you're living the life of your dreams. To lead a happy and fulfilling life, you need to have a crystal-clear vision of what that life looks like.

Let me share my own journey. I've always been a positive, motivated individual. However, there was a time when I felt like I was living someone else's life, a "good" life on paper but unsatisfying on the inside. I called this phase my "quarter-life crisis." Back then, my life might have seemed impressive to outsiders – a well-paying job, a beautiful husband, a house, amazing young adult kids, and an enviable shoe collection. I traveled the world and seemed to have it all. Yet deep inside, I felt like a stranger in my own life. I didn't like my job, my inner life felt empty, and my shoe obsession was nothing more than a way to numb my unhappiness. It dawned on me that I was living a life that I hadn't consciously crafted. While some aspects of it were a result of hard work, others had just happened. I realized that if I wanted a more fulfilling life, I had to stop waiting for things to change and start intentionally creating the life I desired. I embarked on a journey to reimagine my life.

Change didn't happen overnight, but over the years, I transformed from a stable job to securing six-figure contracts on my terms. I started working with people I enjoyed rather than being forced to enjoy people I felt like tolerated each other but would step on each other to get ahead. We moved to a different city and made significant personal transformations. My life became more fulfilling and aligned with my true desires. The first lesson to remember is that a happy and fulfilling life doesn't occur by accident; it's an intentional creation. It's not a one-time process, and I've managed to avoid a midlife crisis by continually assessing and adapting my life to stay happy.

As I approached the next phase of my life, which involved being empty nesters, I realized that my corporate career wasn't in harmony with my future vision. So, I went back to the drawing board to reevaluate my life and make necessary changes to maintain happiness and fulfillment. I then began planning to step away from the corporate world, pursued a professional coaching certification, and became a marriage coach with my husband Brian. Life was good, but when we decided to retire, we started thinking again about what was next. So, once again, I intentionally redesigned my life.

Looking back at the 25 years since my quarter-life crisis, I can say that I'm deeply content with my life. It's not perfect, and there are things I could change, but it's happy and fulfilling because I've set the intention for it to be so. Setting an intention isn't a one-time deal. You need to consistently make decisions that support your intentions and bring them to life.

Now, it's essential to let go of the idea of achieving perfection. Many people spend their lives chasing perfection, only to end up disillusioned when they don't find it. Perfection is an illusion; there's no need to be perfect to have a happy and fulfilling life. Focus on what truly matters to you. In a rich and rewarding life, there are ups and downs, good and bad days. Instead of fixating on what you can improve or change, shift your focus to what's already good in your life.

Your values are your soul's DNA, shaping your character and influencing your life choices. Identifying your values is vital for understanding what truly matters to you. Dig deep to understand your specific values, as they provide clarity about what you want and why you don't want certain things in your life.

For many, they've never given much thought to their values, even though they can recite their company's values. To create your best life, you must know what matters most. Values provide the foundation for setting your intentions. They help you recognize what truly fulfills you.

I urge you not to wait to live your best life. Don't delay your most profound hopes and dreams for some distant future or ideal conditions. Bring your future closer to your present by incorporating small aspects of your ideal life today. Whether it's adding fresh flowers to your home, exploring diverse cuisines, or making simple changes that align with your vision, these actions can profoundly impact your present life and motivate you to pursue your ideal future.

Lastly, take full responsibility for creating your best life. Don't wait for happiness to find you; commit to creating it. While it may seem daunting to realize that you're solely responsible for your life, it's also empowering. Understand what you don't want from life but don't dwell on it. Concentrate on your vision and the plan to make it a reality.

Shift your focus from goals to intentions. This doesn't mean abandoning goals but rather placing them as tools to help you achieve your true intentions. When your intentions are clear, you'll have a deeper sense of commitment, confidence, and clarity. Make the commitment each day to create the life you desire, and you'll move steadily towards your most brilliant life.

Now, let me share Dante's inspiring journey as we wrap up our seven-step mindset makeover. Dante, a seasoned entrepreneur in his mid-40s, embarked on this transformational journey to explore his pivotal "Aha!" moments from Step seven: "See into the Future."

One of Dante's key realizations was that there's no such thing as a perfect life, which means he should aim for an authentic and fulfilling one instead. With our mindset makeover concluding, Dante's commitment to Step seven has been remarkable. He's set his intentions, and his plan includes revisiting Step one, reevaluating, and modifying elements of his life to ensure he's on track to live his best life. Dante understands that these transformations won't spontaneously happen; they require purposeful effort.

The notion of chasing perfection has plagued Dante, often leaving him disillusioned and unfulfilled, especially when driven by financial metrics. He recognizes that his core values are not solely tied to financial success. As a self-proclaimed perfectionist, he had wanted everything to align precisely as planned. Though he achieved milestones like owning a successful publishing company, something vital was missing. Step seven allowed him to refocus on what truly matters.

Dante identified five clear intentions and homed in on his primary values—family, friends, and loved ones, and quality time with them. He understood that the pursuit of these simple, meaningful things is what brings genuine happiness to life. Chasing the illusion of perfection only led him astray. Living with intention and clarity about what he wants is now guiding Dante toward a more fulfilling life.

As we approach the conclusion of our seven-step mindset makeover, let's recap the most vital lessons from Step seven, "See into the Future":

1. Living your best, most brilliant life requires intention; it won't happen by chance.
2. There's no such thing as a perfect life, so relinquish the pursuit of perfection.
3. Take time to understand your values, those things that matter most to you.
4. Get clear about what you don't want to avoid wasting time chasing the wrong goals.
5. Dispel the myth that your goals are the ultimate destination; instead, focus on your intentions.
6. Don't postpone happiness for an ideal future day; make small, immediate changes to bring your vision to life.
7. Remember that you are solely responsible for your life, and you have the power to create your best, most brilliant life.

You've got this, and I believe you're now equipped to embark on your journey to your most brilliant life with intention and purpose. Cheers to the magnificent road ahead!

Make Up of the Brain – Lipstick Shift

To help you set clear intentions and goals

Not setting clear intentions and goals can hurt people by:

1. **Lack of Direction:** Without clear goals, individuals may feel aimless and uncertain about what they want to achieve in life, leading to a lack of purpose and motivation.
2. **Wasted Time and Effort:** Without specific intentions, time and energy may be wasted on activities that don't align with one's aspirations, hindering personal growth and success.
3. **Low Motivation:** The absence of clear goals can result in reduced motivation and a sense of disconnection from one's desires, making it challenging to stay focused and driven.
4. **Missed Opportunities:** Clear goals provide a roadmap for seizing opportunities

and making the most of one's potential. Without them, individuals may overlook chances for growth and improvement.
5. **Increased Stress:** The uncertainty caused by not setting clear intentions and goals can lead to anxiety and stress as people grapple with the ambiguity of their future.

In summary, not setting clear intentions and goals can lead to a lack of direction, wasted resources, low motivation, missed opportunities, and increased stress. It's essential to define objectives and aspirations to guide one's actions and achieve personal fulfillment.

There isn't a specific brain mechanism that prevents people from setting clear intentions and goals, but there are cognitive and psychological factors that can contribute to a lack of clear goal setting. These factors can include:

1. **Procrastination and Avoidance:** The brain's prefrontal cortex, responsible for executive functions like planning and decision-making, can become overwhelmed

when faced with setting goals, leading to procrastination or avoidance.
2. **Fear of Failure:** The brain's amygdala, involved in processing emotions, can trigger fear and anxiety associated with setting ambitious goals. This fear of failure can deter individuals from setting clear intentions and goals.
3. **Comfort Zones:** Humans naturally seek comfort and routine. The brain's basal ganglia plays a role in this by reinforcing established habits. Setting new goals often means stepping outside of one's comfort zone, which the brain may resist.
4. **Low Self-Esteem:** Negative self-beliefs can discourage people from setting clear goals because they may not believe in their ability to achieve them.
5. **Decision Overload:** The brain can be overwhelmed by too many choices. If individuals have numerous potential goals, they may struggle to select one and fail to set clear intentions.

While the brain doesn't prevent goal setting, these cognitive and psychological factors can create barriers that must be consciously overcome to establish clear intentions and goals. Developing strategies and routines to counteract these challenges can be helpful in this regard.

3 Practical Exercises – Fresh Face Forward

To help you set clear intentions and goals

Create a Personal Advisory Board:
- Exercise: Identify the specific areas where you could benefit from guidance, advice, or expertise to help you achieve your aspirations. Determine what kind of advisory roles you'll need. For example, they might require a mentor for career guidance, a health and wellness coach, a relationship counselor, or a financial advisor.
- Strategy: The Personal Advisory Board exercise helps individuals gain valuable insights, perspectives, and support to refine and execute their aspirations. It also holds them accountable for their intentions by involving a trusted network of advisors.

Vision Board Creation:
- Exercise: Encourage individuals to create a vision board by collecting images, words, and symbols that represent their future aspirations and goals. They can arrange these on a physical board or create a digital version.
- Strategy: Visualizing their aspirations through a vision board provides a powerful daily reminder of their intentions, making their goals feel more tangible and achievable.

Visualization Exercise:
- Exercise: Find a quiet, comfortable space and close your eyes. Imagine your ideal future in vivid detail. What do you see, hear, feel, and experience in this future? Picture your aspirations realized.
- Strategy: Regularly practicing this visualization exercise helps create a clear mental image of your goals, making them feel more achievable and motivating you to work towards them.

These practical exercises can help you clarify your intentions and set clear, achievable goals. Remember to work with your coach to ensure the goals are meaningful and relevant to your individual needs and desires. If you haven't gotten help yet, reach out to my team at michellegines.online for more information on getting the roadmap to where you want to go.

"The Fresh Face Forward Mirror"

The final piece inside Michelly's amazing makeup bag, where each product held transformative powers, there was a mirror with a unique name: "The Fresh Face Forward Mirror." This mirror had the extraordinary ability to help Michelly dive into the power of setting clear intentions and goals.

Michelly had always been full of dreams and ideas, but she often found herself drifting through life without a clear sense of direction. She longed for a way to focus her energy and take purposeful steps towards her aspirations.

One morning, as she reached for her makeup bag, she noticed the Fresh Face Forward Mirror glowing with an inviting radiance. She gazed into the mirror, and as her reflection came into view, she felt a compelling sensation of clarity and purpose.

In the days that followed, Michelly began using the mirror as a tool for setting clear intentions and goals. Every morning, she would look into the mirror and visualize her goals, painting a vivid picture of her future. The mirror seemed to respond, reflecting her visions with an ethereal glow.

With the Fresh Face Forward Mirror as her guide, Michelly learned to set intentions and goals that were specific, measurable, and actionable. She no longer allowed her dreams to remain vague and undefined. Instead, the mirror inspired her to articulate her aspirations and create a roadmap to achieve them.

As time passed, Michelly saw a transformation in her life. She no longer drifted aimlessly, unsure of her path. She had a clear sense of direction and knew the steps she needed to take to realize her dreams. The Fresh Face Forward Mirror had become her compass, pointing her toward a future full of purpose and intention.

In the end, the Fresh Face Forward Mirror wasn't just a cosmetic but a powerful tool for setting clear intentions and goals. It had taught Michelly the importance of defining her aspirations and taking actionable steps towards them. She had unlocked the power of intention, and it had transformed her life into one of focus, determination, and achievement.

Let's Zip it Up

We've arrived at the exciting conclusion of the beauty infused guide to personal growth and seven lessons from our makeup bag in "Girl, Make Up Your Mind!" It's been an incredible journey, and you've acquired seven powerful mindset shifts that will lead you toward a life filled with happiness and fulfillment.

In **Step One**, we began by detoxing your dreams, allowing you to **reclaim the energy** you'd been wasting on unattained dreams. **Step Two** empowered you to **discover your "no" and establish boundaries** that let you confidently say no when needed, without the burden of guilt.

Mastering the art of **choosing your mood** became a reality in **Step Three**. Now, you can set yourself up for a great day every day, regardless of life's challenges. **Step Four** guided you in **ignoring the voices** of negativity, letting go of concerns about what others think and shifting your focus to seize life's opportunities.

Fear was demystified in ***Step Five***, where you learned how to confront your inner enemy. You were able to **Mount Your Mascara**

Step Six allowed you to bid **farewell to your "buts"** by leaving your excuses behind, propelling you forward. And now, in

Step Seven, Fresh Face to the Future you've discovered how to see into the future by **setting clear intentions** about what you truly desire in life.

As we conclude this incredible journey, I want to express my gratitude for joining me on this transformational path. More importantly, I want to commend you for embarking on this journey. It's easy to settle for an ordinary life, to be fine with just "fine" and okay with "okay." But I'm thrilled that you've chosen to rise above that. You've chosen to show up and learn how to craft the mindset you need to make your happiest and most fulfilling life a daily reality.

Remember, you truly deserve to live your best, most brilliant life, not just "someday," but every day. With the valuable lessons from this book, I'm confident that you're well on your way to achieving this. If you're eager to dive even deeper into understanding what it takes to live your most brilliant life, I invite you to explore my bestselling books, audio books, courses, training programs, and speaking engagements at Michellegines.online.

Your journey doesn't have to end here, and your potential is boundless. Here's to living your best, most brilliant life every day and to your incredible future!

Sending Love,

Other Books by Michelle Gines:
Copies available at Michellegines.online

- Don't Say That – Don't talk yourself out of the life you deserve.
- Simply Pray with Brian Gines – made for couples & singles. Includes Devotions and Prayers.
- See Yourself to Be Yourself – A 30 Day Devotional to See Yourself the Way God Sees You.
- Giving Your Intentions Some Attention – The title says it all.
- 7 Keys of Queen: Releasing the Entrepreneurial Woman – The Queen of Sheba shows you how.
- Have You Ever Seen a Cow with Tennis Shoes On? – A confidence booster for kids and adults.

Supports & Services:
Available at Michellegines.online

- Don't Do it Alone. Get Help. MentorMe MG Professional Mentors Network – Connecting Skilled Professionals with Experienced Resources.
- Need Business or Life Coaching? We know the people that can help you.
- It's Hard to Run Your Business When Life's Run Away with Your Brain. Brain fuel can help.
- Want to become a Certified Christian Life Coach? Programs Available
- Contact Michelle@Michellegines.online

Tune In and Loosen Up:
ReImagineYOU Lab Podcast

The space and place to learn, test, try, and say goodbye to doubt and delay. Your host, Michelle Gines, the Re-Imagine Scientist! I'm called to create, cultivate, and collaborate with YOU. The real you, the true you, and the best of YOU - that you haven't realized yet.

In the lab podcast, I'm committed to learning from those that have done it. We test ideas, untangle perspectives, create new hypothesis, try a new approach and commit to saying goodbye to anything that has ever stood in your way. Meet Great Guests. Hear Phenomenal Stories. Be Inspired by Encouraging Words. Join us. Find me on all platforms. Tune in. Every Friday.

www.ingramcontent.com/pod-product-compliance
Lightning Source LLC
Chambersburg PA
CBHW030228100526
44585CB00012BA/373